DREAM CHASERS

LIVING IN PURSUIT OF A GOD-SIZED DREAM

PAULA CASILL

Castle Way Publishing
Valley Stream, NY

Table of
Contents

DREAM

GOD'S DESIGN

❖❖

Dreams are incredible and powerful things. I'm not talking about the dreams that come to us in our sleep – although those can be pretty amazing as well. I'm talking about the dreams that God has placed in our hearts, the desires and passions that run so deep within our souls that they can snatch our breath away when we consider where they might take us. I'm talking about the dreams that we have for a better future, for a life that will make a lasting difference, for meaningful and worthwhile success and achievement.

What do your dreams look like? When you picture your ideal future, what do you see? Do you dream of furthering your education, achieving specific goals, establishing a career or building a successful business? Do you want to find a spouse or raise a family? Do you have a talent or skill that you want to share with other people, or do you dream of finding a platform from which you can make an impact on this world? Maybe you dream of traveling, of exploring, of reaching financial independence, or of playing with your grandchildren when you get older.

These kinds of dreams are not ordinary or insignificant things. In fact, they have the power to completely transform our lives. The dreams that we carry in our hearts are what provoke us to achieve, drive us towards excellence, and empower us to reach for more. They keep us from settling for an average, ordinary existence, and push us into the extraordinary destinies that God has in store for us. After all, no one dreams of disappointment or failure. We dream of achieving the things that will fulfill us, things that will give our lives meaning. Our individual dreams may each look different, but one way or another, we all dream of something more. In that regard, I believe that humanity's need to dream is born of God.

Just look at the very first words that the Lord spoke to Adam and Eve in the garden of Eden:

"Be fruitful and multiply; fill the earth and subdue it; have dominion over the fish of the sea, over the birds of the air, and over every living thing that moves on the earth" (Genesis 1:28b).

These powerful words have been guiding humankind, driving us ever since our Creator first spoke them to us. In His very first interaction with humanity, God gave us dominion, He gave us authority, and He also gave us a command to expand, to multiply, and to grow! We were created to reign, to increase, to fill the earth and to subdue it. God spoke this over us at the very moment of our creation. No wonder human beings have spent all of history pushing to exceed our boundaries, to improve our world, and to leave an impact that lasts beyond our lifetimes.

I firmly believe that the urge to dream, that desire for more is something that the Lord planted in each one of us. It can get mixed up in the baser aspects of our own humanity. But at its core, our need to dream mirrors His own desire to see us achieve great things, to live happy and fulfilled lives, and to thrive during the years that we spend on this earth.

You were created to be a dreamer!

Of course dreams are imperfect things. They may be given to us by God, but we are the ones who ultimately define and pursue them. God's perfect plan for our dreams can therefore be tainted by our own sinful nature, or clouded by our lack of vision. When we attempt to achieve the dreams He gave us without His guidance, we will always end up reaching for the wrong thing, or going about it in the wrong way.

As a result, the people of the world, those who don't know God may dream and strive for things that are empty and shallow. They'll dream of fame, fortune, or power because they believe those things will fulfill them. They dream of conquering and overshadowing others because they believe that such actions are necessary in order to build themselves up. They dream of being the prettiest, the richest, or the most talented, even though those titles are ultimately meaningless, because they believe that those things will make them special.

As growing Christians, however, we are constantly learning what it means to live our earthly lives in light of eternity. As Jesus becomes the center of our focus, we learn not to chase the temporary and meaningless treasures that this world offers. We discover that our ultimate fulfillment only comes from a loving and thriving relationship with Christ. Having Him at the center of our lives is the only thing that fills the nagging void that once existed our hearts. He is what gives us purpose, identity, joy, and peace. He becomes our ultimate fulfillment. Without Jesus, nothing else matters.

This new definition of fulfillment, however, does not negate our need to dream. It simply redefines our priorities. Even as Christians, even when our relationships with Jesus are thriving, the urge to dream never goes away. Our dreams may change after we come to know Christ. Our priorities may shift. But we each still carry a hunger to excel, to achieve, and to leave an impact this world. The difference now is that our dreams, just like our lives, will have Christ at their center.

The desire to dream and the instinct to achieve are God-given traits; and I firmly believe that there is a dream inside of each one of us that is divinely inspired. We are God's instruments, the tools that He uses to accomplish His will on this earth. As such, each of us was born with a purpose, a future, and a destiny to fulfill. God has purposely placed passions and desires in each of our hearts to help guide us to those destinies; and if He has placed them there, then we can trust that it is His intention and desire to see those dreams fulfilled. They are part of our purpose, a piece of the reason that we were born into this specific time and place.

But the thing about dreams, especially those that are God-given, is that they are often bigger, deeper, and more impossible than we can imagine achieving on our own. That makes sense when we realize that they reflect not only our own desires, but also His greater purposes. However, sometimes they are so big, so impossible, so far out of reach that it seems there is no way they could ever become reality. Sometimes we attempt to fulfill our dreams only to find mountain-sized obstacles blocking our path. Sometimes they keys to our successes don't lay in our own hands at all, and as time passes, our circumstances only seem to get worse and our dreams seem to fall farther and farther away.

So what should we do when these dreams that God has given us do not come to pass in the ways that we'd expected?

The simple answer is this: don't give up. Don't settle for being just a dreamer. Instead, become a dream chaser. Allow God to use your dream to develop your character, to build your faith, and to provoke you to action. Continue chasing your dream until you reach it, and trust God to lead you along the way.

As humans we are, by nature, dreamers; but so few of us are actually willing to become dream chasers. We have an idea of where we want to go, of what we want to become;

but many of us are not actively involved in the daily pursuit of those dreams. It takes someone with a special drive and an unflagging passion to push and to strive to achieve a dream, no matter what the opposition looks like, no matter how impossible it seems. But it is precisely those people – the ones who have the character to chase their dreams, and to do it God's way – that end up achieving their goals!

Remember this: you cannot become a failure until you've stopped trying. As long as you are pushing forward, as long as you are chasing after your dreams, every setback, every failed attempt is nothing more than a prelude to your success. It may seem easier, at times, to give up and walk away. But that is not what God wants for you. Taking the easy way out will never leave you happy or fulfilled. In fact, those "forgotten" dreams, the ones that people have laid aside, are among the saddest, most painful losses that human beings ever endure. When the things that once gave us hope die away, it can leave us broken, wounded, and incomplete.

It was never God's intention for any of us to give up on the things that He has offered to us. Those dreams that He's placed in our hearts are there because He intends to see them realized. In fact, even long after we have given up on our own dreams, His purposes and plans for them (and for us) are still very much alive. Even when we are faithless He is still faithful. He is still willing to cause our dreams to come to pass.

Perhaps the best example of this in the Bible can be found in the story of the prophet Elisha and the

Shunammite woman. This woman and her husband had built a special room on top of their house for Elisha to stay in whenever he was passing through their town. Elisha was so moved by their generosity that he wanted to do something to bless them in return. However, when he called the woman and asked her what he could do on her behalf, she claimed that she didn't need anything. It was only after she left that Elisha's servant mentioned that she was childless. Elisha immediately called her back, and the exchange that followed was truly remarkable:

So he said, "Call her." When he had called her, she stood in the doorway. Then he said, "About this time next year you shall embrace a son."

And she said, "No, my lord. Man of God, do not lie to your maidservant!" (2 Kings 4:15-16)

This very simple passage speaks volumes to me about buried dreams, and the plans that God has for them.

This woman had no son. That alone is enough to cause any woman pain, but we have to understand that in her culture during that time, this was more than a personal problem or private disappointment. Childbearing was a wife's main responsibility towards her husband and her tribe, the most important achievement of her life. Failure to give birth was seen as evidence that a woman was cursed. A woman who couldn't have children was considered a disgrace, and she was often publicly scorned, ridiculed, and even shunned by society.

So imagine, if you can, the pain that this woman suffered, knowing that she was incapable of producing an heir for her husband. Now multiply that pain many times over for the public disgrace, the looks and whispers, the speculation about why God was punishing her, and the general disdain that she endured because of her barren womb. Imagine the frustration and shame she felt. Imagine how embarrassing it must have been for her. Imagine the hours, days, and years she must have spent wondering what she had done to suffer such a terrible and public failure as a woman.

Now, considering everything that she had suffered, why do you think that she never uttered a word about this – her greatest need – when the prophet of God came to her and asked what he could do to bless her? With Elisha, one of the greatest miracle-working prophets in the Old Testament, standing in front of her and offering to give her whatever she wanted, she was virtually silent. She claimed that everything in her life was fine.

To me this is such a clear demonstration of this woman's condition, and specifically the state of her dream. The only reason that I can possibly fathom for failing to ask was that she had given up all hope of it ever happening. It had probably been so long since she'd given up on having a son that it no longer seemed even remotely possible. Her heart was so broken, her dream so buried, that it might not have even occurred to her to ask. She had no hope left. All she had was the pain and the scars of a forgotten dream.

It was so bad, in fact, that when Elisha promised her that God would give her a son, her first reaction was to beg him not to lie to her! The pain was so deep, and the dream so seemingly impossible, that she could not imagine God actually giving her the thing that she wanted most in this world. Her first instinct was to assume that it was a lie or a trick. It was simply too good to be true.

Does that sound at all familiar to you? Many of us have been in similar positions at some point in our lives. In the face of unfulfilled longings, of broken and impossible dreams, it becomes easier to bury those things away than to look at them day after day. Rather than enduring the heartache and emptiness that comes with these unanswered prayers, many of us simply shut them up in a place where we never look, pretending that they aren't even there. We do our best to forget the pain and disappointment, even as we carry it with us day by day.

We say we're fine, and on the surface that might even be true. But buried somewhere beneath the face of our daily reality there exists the open wound of an unfulfilled dream. As time passed we may have moved on and given up. But we have never really forgotten.

So when God sends someone to speak life and hope into that dead area of our lives, we recoil just like this woman did, reacting out of fear and disbelief. We do not want to endure another heartache. We would rather reject the words of hope than dare to believe once more and risk the possibility of disappointment.

But one of my favorite things about God is His constant attentive awareness of our every thought, dream, and desire. God knows about the things we dream of. He knows about the things we've lost. He knows about the areas where we've tried and failed. And the amazing thing is that He doesn't forget! The passage of time and the accumulation of dust don't diminish His awareness of our pain or our lack. He does not give up or move on. He is always there, waiting for the perfect moment to fill the void in our lives. He is waiting to awaken our dreams!

That's what makes Genesis 1:2-3 one of my favorite passages in the Bible. It says: *And the earth was without form, and void; and darkness was upon the face of the deep. And the Spirit of God moved upon the face of the waters. And God said, "Let there be light:" and there was light.*

There was the earth – formless, lifeless, dark, and empty. There was nothing there. It was void. But even then the Spirit of God was present, hovering, waiting, and poised to make a change. With one simple utterance from His mouth, He transformed the very nature of that vacant and empty place. Where no light had ever existed, there was suddenly light. The void was no longer empty! God filled it with His goodness, with His warmth, with His creation. If He did that for the universe, for trees and rocks and water, how much more will He do to fill the voids created in our hearts by the very dreams that He has given us?

Of course, in our void moments it can be so hard to see that way out. We have such trouble imagining the incredible instantaneous change that God can provoke in our empty situations. Yes, we know that all we need is one touch of God's hand, one word from His mouth, but when the waiting seems endless and the darkness is so dark, our knowledge often conflicts with our expectation.

That is exactly where this Shunammite woman found herself when Elisha spoke to her about her child. He promised her that she would have a son. And even though she recognized that he was, indeed, a man of God, it was too much for her to believe that he was telling the truth. She was afraid to even imagine that he was offering her the very thing she wanted most in this world.

Nevertheless, God was faithful to His word, and to this woman. The time had come for her dream to be fulfilled, and not even her fear or doubt could stop Him from blessing her and giving her the desires of her heart:

But the woman conceived, and bore a son when the appointed time had come, of which Elisha had told her (2 Kings 4:17).

What does this story mean to us? I believe that God put this account into His Word to demonstrate to us just how personally He understands the pain of a broken dream, and just how radically He is willing to move in order to redeem those things that we have lost all hope of accomplishing on our own. However, it is also there to remind us that we don't ever need to give up hope. We don't ever need to put ourselves through the pain that this woman endured. If God refuses to give up on our dreams, then we should refuse to give up on them as well. This story is here to remind you that you don't need to let time, disappointment, fear, or rejection stop you from chasing your God-given dreams.

Before you go any further into this book, I would like you to take some time to revisit the dreams that God has placed in your heart. They may be small and personal, or they may be larger than life. Whatever they look like, take the time now to consider them, to define them, and to write them down. Allow yourself to go back to the dreams that you've forgotten, the ones that seemed so impossible that you may have even given up on them.

Don't allow yourself to be caught in the trap of the Shunammite woman. Your dreams may not seem any more possible today than they did years ago, but believe me when I tell you God has never forgotten them. They are as alive, as true to Him right now as they have ever been; and in this moment He is calling you to return to your beginnings, to reexamine the dreams that once filled you with hope and with joy. If you look you will find Him there, waiting to breathe new life into those very things that you've left behind.

Today can be a new start for you, if you want it to be. Today can be the first day of a life filled with purpose and hope – one lived in pursuit of something greater. Today you can choose that no matter what happens, no matter what your circumstances look like, you will dare to believe that your dreams can come true, and you will chase after them until you see them accomplished.

But how do we do this? How do we live a life chasing after dreams that are too big, too wonderful or too far out of reach for us to ever achieve on our own? The answer to that question is complicated and multi-faceted. But it has been demonstrated to us throughout the Bible in lives of the many men and women who started off with nothing, and ended up with the very success that we ourselves are searching for. These people – David, Joseph, and Abraham among them – have names that you will recognize. They are figures whom we admire, people that we identify as heroes, victors, and yes – dreamers. Each one stands as an example to us of how we can achieve the greatness to which God has called us.

This book that you are about to read is a book about dreams and about dreamers. Specifically, it is about how we as Believers can choose to chase after our dreams in a godly way, ensuring that we are properly positioned for the fulfillment of the dreams that God has placed in our hearts.

Throughout the pages of this book we will learn about the men and women of the Bible who lived their lives in active pursuit of a God-given dream. These people were not perfect. Their lives were not ideal. They all endured hardship, opposition, and disappointment while chasing their dreams. Some of them made mistakes that held them back for a time. Many waited for years without seeing any hope of progress. But at the end of their stories, each one found God to be faithful. Even though their dreams seemed impossible to achieve, He always made a way. He made the impossible possible in each one of their lives. Not only did they each experience the personal victory of a dream fulfilled, but they also played pivotal roles in God's greater plan to bless His people. If God will do that for them, He will do it for us as well!

These people's lives give us hope. They give us inspiration. Most importantly, however, they provide us with a pattern – with principles to follow and a lessons to learn. The very fact that their stories have been preserved in the Bible indicates to us that there are spiritual truths that we can glean from their lives and apply to the pursuit of our own dreams today.

There are seven different principles that I hope you will take away from this book and use for yourself as you chase your own personal dream. Each principle has been demonstrated and lived out in the successes and setbacks along the journeys of the Bible's biggest dreamers. It's time for us to apply them to ourselves as well!

First, we will learn that when God gives us a dream, He intends to use it not only to bless us, but to bless others as well. Our dreams are not ours alone. They are part of a larger story. God designed them to touch and transform the lives of people we may never meet. He wants to use our dreams to bless the nations and to draw them to Him. When we understand this, it will become clear that we must always be willing to give God access to our dreams. We must be willing to adapt and change, to expand our vision until the scope of our dream matches God's greater plan.

Second, we will see that we will never succeed in achieving our God-given dreams if we seek to reach them by carnal, worldly, or sinful means. Realizing this truth will protect us when we are tempted with the opportunity to compromise our spiritual integrity for the sake of our dreams. Remember that God is the one who gave you the dream. He will provide you with the means to achieve it, and that provision will always be true to His nature and His character. Attempting to chase our dreams through ungodly methods will only hurt and delay us in the end, because it will take us off of the path that God has prepared to lead us into our destinies.

Third, we will be reminded that we can never let the passage of time or the size of our opposition dull our passion or our zeal for achieving the dreams in our hearts. In other words, we can never allow ourselves to give up. Even if our natural circumstances indicate that our dreams are out of reach, we must always be willing to try. It is vitally important that we remember that our Almighty God is on our side. He is the one pushing us forward and leading us into our promises. With Him on our side there is nothing that can stand against us. We must strive to maintain this victorious perspective at all times, so that when our dream is placed in front of us we will not hesitate to take hold of it.

Fourth, we will look at the responsibility that we hold to work ahead of time to prepare both ourselves and our situations for the eventual fulfillment of our dreams. We serve a "suddenly" God. We can never be sure when He will present us with an open door, with an opportunity to leap forward into our destinies. It is therefore our responsibility to take action today, and to do all that we can now in preparation for that moment. If we make sure to work and act every day as if our dreams were coming tomorrow, we will find that when they do come, we will be ready to achieve them.

Fifth, we will be challenged to take full advantage of the unexpected opportunities that God gives us in order to boldly pursue the path to our dreams. God will often move in our lives in sudden, amazing, and unusual ways. When He does, He expects us to be willing to take risks and to step outside of our comfort zones in order to achieve His purposes. It can be difficult in those moments to obey and to follow where He is leading. It may even be frightening. But we cannot allow fear and timidity to hold us back. If we are following after God, and if we are willing to step out in faith, He will not allow us to be ashamed. He will always lead us to victory.

Sixth, we will study a poignant reminder of just how important it is too keep our faith and our confidence firmly planted on Jesus – the One who gave us our dreams to begin with. Remember that these dreams that burn within your heart are His dreams. He has a plan to fulfill them, and He has never failed. So even when things look like they're going wrong, even when your dreams seem impossibly out of reach, you should never give up hope. Your circumstances today can not define your tomorrow unless you let them. When your confidence is firmly planted in your relationship with God you will never be put to shame, no matter what trials may come.

And finally, we will look at the power and perseverance that comes with an attitude of expectation. If we know that our dreams come from God, we will be able to live every day of our lives as if we expect Him to fulfill them. That expectation, that persistent and determined assurance that

He will come through will keep us ever vigilant – ever watchful for the hand of God that is coming to move on our behalf.

We serve a God of dreamers. If He has placed a dream within you, you can rest assured that He intends to fulfill it. The dreams that He gives us are there for a purpose, and when we are submitted to His leading and willing to do things His way, we will see Him move in amazing and often miraculous ways in order to make our dreams come to pass.

So let this be the first step on a new journey. Allow yourself to be open to God's leading and His instruction. And as you move forward, challenge yourself to dig deeper and to push harder. Dare to live a life beyond the boundaries of what the world says is possible. Permit yourself to believe that the Lord has called you to greater things. Allow your dream to drive you. Become a dream chaser, a man or woman who is in constant pursuit of the dreams that God has given you. Do that, and you will find yourself living the life you've always dreamed of.

EXPAND

HANNAH'S SURRENDER

❖❖

One of the first things that we need to understand about the dreams that God has given us is this simple truth: that they are about more than our personal fulfillment. That might seem a little counter-intuitive at first. After all, we tend to dream in very personal ways, reaching for things that will enrich our own lives. We expect our dreams to satisfy us, to bless us, and to make our lives better.

There's nothing wrong with that, of course. But it's really only the smallest portion of what our dreams were made to do. You see, God has planted these dreams in our hearts with a larger vision in mind. He wants to use our lives to change the world, to build His kingdom, and to bring Him glory; but that only happens when we willingly give those dreams back to Him, so that He can use them for His will.

Please understand that I'm not trying to say that we shouldn't dream for things that will bless us in a personal way. Of course we should! God wants us to be blessed. He wants us to prosper. He wants us to have fulfillment and joy while we are on this earth. But there is a greater cause, a higher purpose towards which He is working, and even the seemingly small and personal dreams that God has given us are always a part of His larger plan to reach out to the people around us. Of course His plans will always bless us, but He wants to use us and our dreams to extend His blessing to others as well.

Your dreams have the power to bless other people!

So many Christians are afraid of dreaming for big things, or for reaching towards the big dreams that they already have in their hearts, because deep down they are scared that God doesn't want them to succeed. They imagine that their personal fulfillment will somehow conflict with God's design for their lives.

But when we understand that God is the one who gave us our dreams, and that He wants to use them to advance His kingdom, our perspective will change. Instead of seeing our personal dreams as something separate from God's plan, we will begin to discover how He has merged the two into a single beautiful tapestry. As we grow in this understanding, as we see our dreams through God's perspective, it will cause our dreams to grow and expand as well. They will begin to look more and more like the vision that He has for our lives. In fact, we will often find that the largest, most unbelievable and far-reaching dreams that we can imagine achieving are only a fraction of what the Lord has in store for us.

Even the prophet Isaiah had to make this journey. Even he needed God to expand his dream. He understood that God had created him for a powerful purpose. But at first he wasn't able to imagine the lengths to which God wanted to use him. When he spoke about his dream, his calling, Isaiah said:

"Listen, O coastlands, to Me, and take heed, you peoples from afar! The Lord has called Me from the womb; From the matrix of My mother He has made mention of My name ...

And He said to me, 'You are My servant, O Israel, in whom I will be glorified.'

Then I said, 'I have labored in vain, I have spent my strength for nothing and in vain; yet surely my just reward is with the Lord, and my work with my God'"
(Isaiah 49:1, 3-4).

Isaiah knew that God chose him to accomplish something powerful. He had a dream that was bigger than most – he dreamt of bringing the nation of Israel to repentance, of drawing them back to an authentic relationship with their Lord. He understood that God intended to glorify Himself through his life and ministry, and he was actively chasing after this dream with all that he had. However, in these verses he was complaining that his work in that area seemed to be fruitless. He knew that his dream was from God, but his labor had produced no results. His dream was not yet fulfilled.

"Indeed He says, 'It is too small a thing that You should be My Servant to raise up the tribes of Jacob, and to restore the preserved ones of Israel; I will also give You as a light to the Gentiles, that You should be My salvation to the ends of the earth'" (Isaiah 49:6).

God's response to Isaiah's complaint was to expand his vision even further, to make it even larger. It didn't matter that Isaiah had not yet seen any success; as far as God was concerned his problem was that he wasn't reaching far enough. Here in this very passage God called Isaiah to move beyond what he had once considered to be his wildest ambitions, his greatest aspirations. God told him to dream bigger.

Isaiah was a man who was already willing to chase a big dream. He started off by saying, "Look at me, God created me to do great things!" He considered himself a voice to the nation of Israel, the one who would bring the people of God back into unity. But even though he was chasing after a grand and lofty goal, God still had so much more waiting for him. The Lord told him that the dream he had was too small a thing. It simply wasn't enough! God needed Isaiah to expand his dreams until they matched up with the vision that He had for Isaiah's life!

The Lord has more in store for you than you have ever dared to dream or imagine. This isn't hype, it's not ego-boosting, it's solid Biblical truth. You may think that these "special" and "important" callings are reserved for a chosen few, but you'd be wrong. When Jesus spoke to his disciples about their purpose, their abilities, and their potential he was speaking to all of them without exception. When He told them that they could do greater works on this earth than the ones that He did, He spoke of *he who believes in Me ... (John 14:12b)*. That includes you!

You are more capable than you give yourself credit for. You can reach farther than you've ever imagined. You have the power of God inside of you, a power that can do more than your mind can comprehend. Therefore whenever you allow a dream to shrink, whenever your vision becomes centered on your life and boxed in by your individual expectations, whenever you limit your dream to something that will bless only yourself or your personal circle of influence, you run the risk of doing what Isaiah did. You risk missing the larger picture that God is painting.

We cannot be a people who dream with blinders on. We must not allow our focus to remain so narrow that we miss the broader understanding of what God intends to do through us. Dreaming in this limited manner is one of the easiest ways for us to derail ourselves from the greater purpose to which we have been called.

There is a very clear example of this simple mistake in the story of Hannah. She is the first dreamer in the Bible whose journey we will study. As we examine her story we will discover a very valuable lesson about dreams that we can apply to our own lives. We will see from her example that we must be willing to expand our vision and to embrace

God's greater plan for our dreams, because doing so opens the door for Him to move on our behalf.

Now there was a certain man of Ramathaim Zophim, of the mountains of Ephraim, and his name was Elkanah the son of Jeroham ... And he had two wives: the name of one was Hannah, and the name of the other Peninnah. Peninnah had children, but Hannah had no children (1 Samuel 1:1a, 2).

Hannah was a relatively ordinary Israelite woman who lived a relatively ordinary life. But like the Shunammite woman we discussed earlier, Hannah had a serious personal problem. She wasn't able to bear children. And just like the Shunammite, the one thing Hannah wanted more than anything was a child to call her own. She was chasing the simplest of dreams, one that was nevertheless completely out of her reach. She wanted to bear a son.

Childbearing, it should be noted, is an incredibly powerful symbol and a beautiful analogy for the realization of a dream. The parallels are obvious. Just like with children, the seeds of our dreams' potential already exist within us. Like children, dreams are incredibly personal; they are a product of who we are. They are our legacy, our gift to the world, and among the greatest joys in our lives. We cherish them, love them, plan for them, draw purpose from them, and yearn for them – and all of these things begin within us long before they ever arrive.

So when, like Hannah, we find ourselves in a place of barrenness – when we are unable to bring our dreams into reality, that disappointment can become a defining part of who we are. It is an emptiness that we cannot fill, a void that we cannot deny. The lack of life, the lack of fruit, is a terrible thing to endure.

Hannah understood this pain. It was especially real to her because her barrenness was not only figurative; it was literal as well. Her inability to realize her dream was a direct result of a naturally barren womb. And as we discussed in the last chapter, the society that she lived in considered any married woman who could not bear children to be cursed.

Hannah would have been scorned and ridiculed by many members of her community. But as if that weren't enough of a burden, she was also forced to endure that same type of abuse in her own home. Hannah had a rival in her family named Peninnah, and Peninnah made Hannah's life miserable. She was Elkanah's other wife, and she also happened to have the very thing that Hannah wanted most – children.

To our modern perspective the idea of having to share a husband sounds trying enough. But you can't help but feel especially bad for Hannah, who had to share her husband with a woman who was able to give him that very essential and special "something" that Hannah could not.

Peninnah's success was an unavoidable part of Hannah's daily reality. These two women could not get away from one another if they'd tried. They probably lived in the same house, which meant that Hannah would have seen Peninnah and spoken to her every day. They would have shared chores, decisions, and responsibilities. Their lives were inexorably tied to one another. Hannah had no way to escape the presence of the woman who was living her dream. Her daily life was filled with constant reminders of her own failures.

Imagine what frustration Hannah must have felt as she watched her rival giving birth, nursing her children, and caring for them as they grew. Imagine the bitterness that she must have experienced while washing Peninnah's children's clothes, cleaning up their messes, or making their beds. Hannah had a lot to endure, and this wasn't even the worst of it:

And her rival also provoked her severely, to make her miserable, because the Lord had closed her womb. So it was, year by year, when she went up to the house of the Lord, that she provoked her; therefore she wept and did not eat (1 Samuel 1:6-7).

It's amazing to me how easily we gloss over a verse like this. But I'd like you to take the time to carefully consider what the Bible is telling us here about Hannah's situation. It says that Peninnah actual provoked Hannah. That means that she did and said things to intentionally make her suffer. She took advantage of the fact that she had children and Hannah did not, and she used it to shame and torment her.

I don't want to spend too much time on focusing Hannah's problems, but I do want to make sure that you have an understanding of exactly where she was and what she was suffering, because although her situation seemed extreme, it is probably registering as familiar to some of you. You may also be struggling with watching another person live out the dream that is closest to your heart. You may have spent time wondering why God would give them the one thing you want most, while holding it back from you.

You are not alone.

Every day that Hannah woke up she knew that she was going to have to face Peninnah with her stinging words and nasty comments. Every day she knew that the woman who had everything that she'd ever wanted was waiting for her, looking for a chance to provoke her further. There was no peace for Hannah, no escape from this awful woman – not even in her own home. Can you imagine having to live a life like that?

For years this went on. It wasn't a short season in Hannah's life. And as you might imagine, the torture, the frustration, and the disappointment took its toll.

Then Elkanah her husband said to her, "Hannah, why do you weep? Why do you not eat? And why is your heart grieved? Am I not better to you than ten sons?"
(1 Samuel 1:8)

Hannah's situation eventually deteriorated to such a terrible place the she could no longer even bring herself to eat. She was so filled with grief, so empty and desperate, that even the unconditional love of her husband was no longer enough to bring her joy.

I pray that you have never found yourself in Hannah's position, in a place of such despair that even the most fulfilling aspects of your life feel hollow and incomplete. But even if that is exactly where you are today, you do not need to give up hope. Your story isn't over. In fact, just like Hannah's, it has really only just begun!

You see, it's easy to look at Hannah's life and wonder why she had to endure such suffering and pain. It's easy to look at her unfulfilled dream, her barren womb, and conclude that something somewhere had gone terribly wrong. We might assume, as the people in her circle of influence probably did, that Hannah had done something especially evil or sinful to deserve such a curse. Or we might be inclined to think that God just didn't care about Hannah's dream, that it was outside of His will or beneath His attention.

But the truth is that Hannah hadn't done anything evil. She wasn't an unusually sinful woman. And God wasn't leaving her there, stuck in an impossible situation, because He'd forgotten about her or because He enjoyed watching her suffer. In fact, as we will discover soon enough, He was even more invested in seeing Hannah's dream come to pass than she was!

Before that could happen, however, God needed Hannah to come to a place where she was ready to make a radical decision. This terrible circumstance in which she found herself was nothing more than the last step along the journey that she had to take in order to arrive at the moment of her miracle:

And she was in bitterness of soul, and prayed to the Lord and wept in anguish. Then she made a vow and said, "O Lord of hosts, if You will indeed look on the affliction of Your maidservant and remember me, and not forget Your

maidservant, but will give Your maidservant a male child,
then I will give him to the Lord all the days of his life, and
no razor shall come upon his head" (1 Samuel 1:10-11).

Finally Hannah reached the point where she could not endure her suffering any longer. She was bitter. She was in anguish. She was so upset that she couldn't even pray out loud. I would be surprised if she had any hope left in her heart. She must have felt like she would not survive much longer with the pain of this unfulfilled dream pressing on her soul. In that broken, desperate condition she came into the house of God and made a vow to the Lord that changed absolutely everything. She promised God that if He would answer her prayer, if He would give her a son, then she would return that boy back to Him to serve Him all the days of his life.

In that moment, with that simple prayer, Hannah's life was transformed. After years of suffering at the hands of her rival, after years of barrenness, emptiness, and pain, Hannah finally made a life-altering choice. She decided to give her dream, her son, up to God.

That vow held incredible power. Hannah was begging God to give her the one things she wanted most in this world, and in the same breath promising that she would not keep it. It was an extreme thing to say, an extreme decision to make. She was willing to surrender her dream to the Lord, if only He would let her see it fulfilled.

It is hard to imagine the incredible pressure, the sheer desperation that could drive a woman to make such a pledge. But it cannot be denied that those words moved the hand of the Lord. He heard her cries, and as she was leaving the temple that day, the priest Eli reassured her that her words had not fallen on deaf ears:

Then Eli answered and said, "Go in peace, and the God of Israel grant your petition which you have asked of Him."

And she said, "Let your maidservant find favor in your sight." So the woman went her way and ate, and her face was no longer sad (1 Samuel 1:17-18).

I find it incredible that this one simple encounter with God was enough to change Hannah's demeanor so completely. She walked into the tabernacle so tortured, so hopeless that she couldn't manage to eat, or even speak her prayers out loud, but she walked out knowing that her future was about to change.

That's a truly remarkable transformation, given the circumstances. After all, it's not as though she had a visitation by an angel. No voice boomed out from heaven to promise her a son. Even Eli's words were vaguely encouraging at best. He didn't speak to her prophetically and tell her that she was going to give birth. In fact, there was nothing at all about Hannah's natural circumstances that changed in the time that she spent before the Lord.

And yet, it cannot be denied that Hannah walked out of that tabernacle radically altered. Her demeanor was different. Her perspective had changed. She suddenly had hope! It didn't happen because of an external encounter. It happened because of an internal transformation.

Hannah made the quality decision on that day that her dreams were no longer in her own hands. She surrendered her passion up to God, to do with it as He would. I believe that her simple but profound promise was the very act that gave her the release that she so desperately sought. Even though nothing had changed in the natural realm, on a spiritual level at least, she must have understood that she had just precipitated her own breakthrough. No wonder she felt empowered!

After all of her suffering, after all of the fruitless and frustrating days that she spent stuck in a hopeless situation, Hannah had finally found hope. The only thing that she had done differently was to decide to fully surrender her future to the will of God. His plan was now her plan. Her future was entirely in His hands. She was no longer even the beneficiary of her own deepest desires. Her heart's desire had once been to have a son. Now it was to give that son to the Lord so that he could live a life in His service.

The result of all of this was that she was finally aligned with the greater plan that God had in store for her. She could not know it at the time, at least not in any concrete or natural way, but that simple shift was all that God was waiting for. As soon as she surrendered her dream up to Him, He instantly opened her womb and gave her the son that she had so desperately wanted. Her dream became her reality!

So it came to pass in the process of time that Hannah conceived and bore a son, and called his name Samuel, saying, "Because I have asked for him from the Lord"
(1 Samuel 1:20)

Here, at the end of Hannah's story, we are finally able to see the reason that her dream had been delayed for as long as it was. In this simple verse, we are shown why God had to wait for Hannah to surrender her son to Him before He could bless her. Hannah's son, the fulfillment of her dream, was no ordinary child. She gave birth to a boy named Samuel – the same Samuel who was destined to spend his life as the spiritual leader of the entire nation of Israel.

This is the same Samuel who would eventually anoint Saul, and later David, as the first kings of Israel. This is the Samuel who spoke the word of the Lord with authority and uncompromising zeal in a time when the Israelites were more interested in assimilating the ideas and cultural norms of the nations surrounding them. This Samuel lived his life as a beacon of light in a time of spiritual darkness. He was one of the greatest prophets that Israel ever knew. There are two books of the Bible that are not only named after him, but dedicated to chronicling the incredible transformation that took place in the nation of Israel under his leadership. His life left a mark on the people of God that lasted for untold generations.

Samuel – this world changing man of God – was the product of Hannah's dream, the fruit of her once-barren womb. With that understanding, we cannot help but wonder what would have happened if Hannah had not been willing to make her vow. What would the world have missed if, instead of growing up in the house of the Lord, Samuel had stayed with his mother and grown up to live an ordinary life?

All of Hannah's suffering, all of her years of emptiness were a necessary thing. They brought her to the place of surrender, the place where she needed to be so that God could not only bless her, but use her to bless so many more.

This is the first lesson that we must learn if we want to live our lives in successful pursuit of the dreams that God has given us. These dreams that we cherish, that we long for – they are meant to be much larger than we realize. Their impact on this world is far greater than our limited scope of understanding can fathom. God wants to use us in ways that are more exhilarating, more far-reaching than we would dare to imagine. But in order to see these dreams come to pass, we first need to make sure that we are fully aligned with His greater vision. God placed these dreams in our hearts to be a blessing to us, but as long as we are trying to maintain control of that blessing, as long as we are unwilling to give our dreams back to Him, we run the risk of being as stuck and as miserable as Hannah was.

So if you have a dream in your heart that you believe is from God, I challenge you today to surrender it back to Him. Don't hold yourself back from receiving your own blessing. Do not be the one who delays your destiny. If you are willing to place your deepest and most passionate desires for your own future into the hands of the Lord, He will do more than open doors. He will produce life where there was once nothing but barrenness.

"For this child I prayed, and the Lord has granted me my petition which I asked of Him. Therefore I also have lent him to the Lord; as long as he lives he shall be lent to the Lord"(1 Samuel 1:27-28a).

Before we end Hannah's story there are two additional points that are worth mentioning, since they are directly applicable to our own lives. The first is this: after Hannah received her miracle, after her dream became a reality, she remembered her prayer and carried through with her vow. As soon as her son was weaned and old enough to live without her, Hannah brought him to the tabernacle and gave him to Eli, the priest, to be raised in the service of the Lord.

Take a moment to think about that, because it might be the most powerful thing that Hannah did through this whole story. Back in her moment of desperation, praying in the tabernacle, Hannah's words had no physical form. She didn't have a son to surrender to God, and she had no tangible evidence that he would ever exist. The sacrifice that she was making was purely theoretical. But after two years had passed, Hannah was faced with the very real, very human consequence of honoring her promise. She had carried Samuel in her womb for nine months. She had nursed him, held him, cared for him, and loved him for another year. She was finally a mother! It seems almost impossible that she would have the strength of character to let go of the very thing that she'd waited so long to receive!

But Hannah had made a promise. She had vowed to God that she would surrender her son to do His work, to serve in the house of the Lord all the days of his life; and her character was so solid that she refused to back down. She would not allow herself to take back what she'd promised to God.

This reminds me of Psalm 15, which has always been one of my favorite passages in the Bible. It starts by asking who can abide in God's tabernacle, and then it begins to describe the characteristics of a righteous and upright man. One of the most practical and telling lines in the Psalm comes at the end of verse 4, where it says: *He who swears to his own hurt and does not change; ... He who does these things shall never be moved (Psalm 15:4b,5b).*

Hannah was such a woman of integrity that she didn't waver or shrink away from her decision to surrender her son to the Lord, and in that way she sets an incredible example for us to follow. Strive to become a man or woman of righteousness, one who will keep your word, and as this Psalm promises, you will never be moved. You will never have anything to fear.

And the Lord visited Hannah, so that she conceived and bore three sons and two daughters. Meanwhile the child Samuel grew before the Lord (1 Samuel 2:24).

The final thing that I would like to point out about Hannah is also my favorite part of the whole story. After years of struggle and disappointment, Hannah came to a place of total surrender. She gave up her dream – her son – for a greater purpose. God heard her prayer, honored her vow, and gave her a child. Still, there is no denying that Hannah's choice was a sacrifice. She did not keep the son that she had spent so long waiting for. She selflessly gave him up to the Lord's service.

However, that sacrifice came with another blessing, in fact it came with several. God did not leave her arms empty for long. Over the course of time Hannah had five more children! None of them could ever replace Samuel, of course. But when she surrendered her first child to God, He made sure that she was not left in lack. He gave her more children, more than she'd ever asked for. He fulfilled her over and over, affirming her time and again, until the piece of her life that had once been barren and empty was filled to overflowing with His abundant life!

That's the incredible thing about surrendering dreams over to the will of God: even when it seems to require sacrifice and loss, He will always turn it around to bless you in a greater measure. He will never leave you empty-handed or unsatisfied. If you will trust Him with your most precious dreams, if you will give them to Him to use according to His plans, He will pour back into your life the very blessings that you think you are giving up.

I want you to take a moment right now and ask yourself a question. Who is the primary beneficiary of your dreams? Is it yourself? Your family? Your closest friend? There's nothing wrong with answering *yes* to those questions. It puts you in exactly the same position as Hannah, and most of the other dreamers out there as well. But just because your dream is small and personal doesn't mean that it can't be used to bless multitudes of people.

Realizing that truth and embracing it is a powerful act that will open countless doors into your future.

God's plan for your dream is bigger than your own, and He will wait with infinite patience until you are ready to give over control of that dream to Him so that He can expand it to its greatest potential. As long as you are clinging to your own control of your dream, you may meet with difficulties and emptiness. You may even end up faced with the provocation of another person who has everything that you want! But God is not allowing these things to happen in order to torture you or even to test you. It is happening because you have a choice to make, and until you make that choice your dream cannot move forward.

To be a dream chaser requires that you first understand and embrace God's heavenly vision for your dream. Until your dream is open to His greater plan, He will not be able to help you fulfill it. So don't live your life on pause any longer. Don't delay your own dream for one more day. Lift your desires up to the Lord. Give Him sway over your future, and He will not only fulfill your dream, He will bring you to places that you'd never imagined.

OBEY

Moses' Big Mistake

❖❖

In the last chapter we learned about how God wants to use our dreams to bless other people. We discovered that our dreams – even the ones that are so personal that they seem knit to our very souls – are a part of God's greater plan, and are as vitally important to Him as they are to us. Our dreams are His dreams, and He wants to see them come to pass just as much as we do! We don't have to convince God to help us reach our goals. He's been trying to lead us towards those dreams from the beginning. All we have to do is surrender them back to His control.

This realization cannot help but have a very practical impact on the way that we live our lives, and specifically on the way that we chase after our dreams. You see, if we believe that our dreams are a part of God's greater plan, if we know that He wants these dreams to come to pass, then we can rest assured that He has orchestrated a plan for us to follow in order to reach them. That means that we don't have to make our own way. We don't have to forge a path on our own. He has already done the work of figuring out how we can get to where He wants us to go. Our responsibility is simply to follow the plan that He has already put in place for us. We just need to follow His lead.

This brings us to the second key to living our lives in successful pursuit of our dreams: if we are going to chase after dreams that are a part of God's plan, then we need to go about doing it His way. If an architect handed you blueprints and instructions and asked you to build a bridge, you would not attempt to skip steps or switch out materials as you went along. You would follow the instructions as closely as possible, because you know that the smallest change could potentially lead to catastrophe. This same principle applies to our lives. God knows how to build our dreams. He knows how to construct a future for us that is beautiful and strong. But His plans can only be realized when we are careful to follow His instructions.

Unfortunately many of us make the mistake of attempting to reach our God-given dreams by ungodly methods. We may have the best of intentions, but along they we make decisions and take actions that contradict or fall short of God's character. When we are faced with an opportunity to "get ahead" by compromising, we can sometimes forget that our God-given dreams cannot be achieved by worldly means. But when we try to use the systems of the world to fulfill our divinely inspired goals, we will ultimately find ourselves frustrated, our dreams out of reach, and our circumstances in a mess.

Of course, we're not the only ones who make that mistake. In fact, some of the greatest men and women in the Bible did the same thing. Moses is one of the most obvious examples of a Biblical hero who fell into this trap – and we are going to spend some time looking at and learning from the mistakes that he made.

When we think of a man like Moses, we generally don't think of failure. He was, after all, a powerful man of God who fulfilled a world-changing destiny. He was actually one of the greatest leaders that the nation of Israel ever knew. He delivered the Hebrew people out of bondage, performing miracles signs and wonders along the way. But Moses did not achieve his success instantly. In fact, as we study his story we will see that his first attempts to deliver his people failed miserably.

We all know how Moses' life began. He was a Hebrew baby who was saved from certain death when his mother placed him in a basket and sent him down the Nile river. While he was floating among the reeds Pharaoh's daughter found him and had compassion on him. She adopted him as her own and brought him into her home.

As a result of this miraculous series of events, Moses grew up as a prince in the land of Egypt. At the time, his people, the Israelites, were living in oppression and slavery. Moses, however, lived a charmed life. He was raised as Pharaoh's grandson, which means that he was not only free from oppression, but he was a man of influence and power. Moses wasn't just ordinary Egyptian, he was a mighty ruler among their people.

Now it came to pass in those days, when Moses was grown, that he went out to his brethren and looked at their burdens (Exodus 2:11a).

The amazing thing about Moses was that even though he was raised as Egyptian royalty, he embraced the fact that he was also a Hebrew. Even though he had been given all of the power of Egypt – an authority that goes beyond anything that we can understand in our modern culture – he never lost sight of the fact that he belonged to the people of God. In fact, the very first thing that the Bible tells us about Moses as an adult was that he went out to the Hebrew slaves to see their suffering. He bore witness to their oppression, and his heart was filled with compassion for them. He wanted to help his people, and he dreamed of finding a way to set them free.

Moses was in the ideal situation of having a dream that he seemed especially suited to achieve. His goal was to deliver the Israelites from their bondage. He wanted to alleviate their suffering. Doing this would not be an easy task, even for someone with his incredible position of authority. But if there was anyone in the entire nation if Egypt who could have made it happen, it was Moses. He was a Hebrew, of course, which made this dream very personal. It would have given him the passion and drive to see the dream through to completion. But he was also a part of Pharaoh's family which gave him a unique and powerful level of influence among the Egyptians. He had the ear of the king, and the social and political sway to do things that would have been impossible for other men.

Unfortunately, however, Moses was never able to put his position or power to good use. Before he could get that far, before he began to chase his dream in earnest, he made a terrible mistake that changed the course of his future:

And he saw an Egyptian beating a Hebrew, one of his brethren. So he looked this way and that way, and when he saw no one, he killed the Egyptian and hid him in the sand (Exodus 2:11b-12).

While visiting with his Hebrew brethren and seeing their suffering first-hand, Moses happened to come across an Egyptian man who was beating on one of the Israelite slaves. In the heat of that moment, believing that he was unobserved, Moses did something that most of us would consider unthinkable: he struck down and killed the Egyptian. He committed murder.

Of course, Moses had reasons for what he did. In fact, it is safe to assume that he considered his actions completely justified. The man that Moses killed was beating one of the very Hebrews that he wanted so desperately to save. It must have hurt him to watch that happening. It must have angered him to see the brutality of it all. In fact, I would imagine that this Egyptian man seemed to be a living symbol of the very oppression that he wanted to end. By killing the Egyptian, Moses probably believed that he was avenging his kinsman. In fact, in a later account of this same story, we are told that he actually considered this murder to be an act of deliverance:

"Now when he was forty years old, it came into his heart to visit his brethren, the children of Israel. And seeing one of them suffer wrong, he defended and avenged him who was oppressed, and struck down the Egyptian. For he supposed that his brethren would have understood that God would deliver them by his hand, but they did not understand" (Acts 7:23-25).

Nevertheless, all the mitigating circumstances, all of the excuses that Moses might have used to justify his actions could not change the fact that what he did was terribly wrong. His actions may have been driven by passion and provoked by injustice, but they were still not excusable. It's no wonder that he felt the need to hide the Egyptian's body and conceal what he had done.

Moses made a terrible mistake in that moment, one that would haunt him and delay his destiny for decades. But his actions provide us with the perfect context in which to discuss a very important lesson. You see, God has already made a way for your dream to become reality. He would not have given it to you if He didn't intend to fulfill it. However, if we truly believe this then we must also recognize that the path that He has made will always be perfectly aligned with His will and His word. God will never give you a dream that can only be realized through dishonest or sinful actions. Therefore, if we are serious about achieving our dreams we must never allow ourselves to pursue them with anything short of absolute moral and spiritual integrity.

This is an important truth, one that we cannot afford to ignore if we expect to move forward into success. It must be firmly implanted in our hearts and minds now – before we arrive at a moment of choice. Because while most of us would never reach the point where we would intentionally kill another human being, we are often confronted with situations in which we must make personal moral decisions that are not so different than the one Moses faced.

When you have a dream that has been given to you by God, you will inevitably encounter situations in which you must choose between doing things God's way, and acting in a way that compromises your integrity – one that feels satisfying in the moment, but falls short of the standard to which you have been called to live. It probably won't be a matter of murder. In fact, it might seem like something completely insignificant and harmless. It will almost certainly be something that feels justifiable in its context. However, any time that we choose wrong over right, sin over righteousness, or compromise over integrity, we are harming our futures and moving ourselves farther from our destinies.

When presented with this decision point, Moses failed. He fell into sin and did the wrong thing. Despite the excuses and justifications that probably played themselves out in his head, he wasn't ignorant of his wrongdoing. In fact, the Bible tells us that he checked before he struck to make sure that there were no witnesses. Then he tried to hide what he did by burying the body in the sand. He clearly did not want his actions to be discovered.

What he did not recognize at the time, however, was that it didn't really matter if anyone else discovered his sin. His ability or inability to hide his actions from natural eyes was, in fact, irrelevant. There was no way that God would be able to work through his compromise. no way that He could liberate His people through Moses' sinful action.

Before we jump to condemn Moses, however, we must remember that his story exists in the Bible for our benefit. It isn't there to give us a chance to point our fingers or shake our heads, but to help us understand the magnitude of weight that our own decision can have on our futures. This story is available to us so that we can learn from it, and so that we can avoid making the same mistakes on our own journeys toward our dreams.

And when he went out the second day, behold, two Hebrew men were fighting, and he said to the one who did the wrong, "Why are you striking your companion?"

Then he said, "Who made you a prince and a judge over us? Do you intend to kill me as you killed the Egyptian?"

So Moses feared and said, "Surely this thing is known!" (Exodus 2:13-14)

The next day Moses did not yet know that his terrible mistake had been discovered. He thought he had gotten away with it. In fact, he was so confident in his secret, so sure of his own reputation that he actually attempted to mediate an argument between two Hebrew men whom he found fighting with each other. He even chastised the one who resorted to physical violence.

So when that man challenged Moses' hypocrisy, it must have come as quite a shock to his system. In that moment Moses realized that the thing that he had tried to hide had come to light. Suddenly the consequences of his rash decision became frighteningly real. He realized that his position, his reputation, his influence, and even his life were all very much at risk. No wonder his first reaction was fear and panic! He must have understood that he had placed himself in a very dangerous position.

What I find especially telling about this scenario, however, was that Moses seemed less concerned with the inherently wrong nature of his actions than he was with the fact that they had become publicly known. In this way, he represents a common attitude when it comes to our human relationship to sin. There are times when people, even Christians, are less concerned with facing and repenting from the sins that they commit than they are about avoiding the consequences that they face when those sins come to light. Nevertheless, Moses' real problems began not when his sin was discovered, but when it was committed in the first place.

As Christians, we also face very serious problems as a result of our sin. For us, the true danger does not always come from the natural consequences of our actions, but from the spiritual ones. Even if no one ever discovers our wrongdoing, even if we are never held accountable while we are on this earth, every action that we take that is contrary to God's will inevitably diverts us from His plans and purposes for our lives. When we sin, we are not only failing to live up to the righteousness of God that now abides within us. We are also removing ourselves from the path that He has set at our feet.

We are, of course, covered by the mercy and the grace of God. He knows that we are not perfect. We will make mistakes, and He is generous in His forgiveness towards us. His blood bought us the righteousness that we could never earn on our own. Nevertheless, as children of God and disciples of Christ we have a very real responsibility to do everything in our power to live our lives according to the pattern that He has set out for us.

When Pharaoh heard of this matter, he sought to kill Moses. But Moses fled from the face of Pharaoh and dwelt in the land of Midian; and he sat down by a well (Exodus 2:15).

Moses' carnal choices ended up having serious carnal consequences. What he had done was wrong not only from God's perspective, but also from the perspective of the rulers of the land; and as a result, it wasn't long before he was being hunted down so that he could face the punishment for his crime. He was, after all, a murderer. His rationalization of that murder, as justified as it may have seemed to him, could not protect him from the arm of the law. The only way for him to escape the situation with his life was to flee the country and go into hiding.

This demonstrates yet another reason why it so damaging for us to attempt to achieve our dreams by corrupted natural means. We can never tell what terrible unforeseen consequences our actions may trigger. Of course it's easy to argue from an objective perspective that Moses shouldn't have been all that surprised by the repercussions of his wrongdoing. But I think it's safe to imagine that if he'd known for certain what he would endure as a result of his murderous rage, he would have stopped short of killing that Egyptian.

That's the problem with sin. We think we can get away with it. We imagine that we can manage the fallout. We have no way of looking into our own futures and seeing the consequences of our choices, and so we talk ourselves into believing that they will be small, insignificant, or maybe even nonexistent. But that's not the way sin works. Even when we are unable to see the specific results of our actions, we have this guarantee: that anything we do to compromise our spiritual integrity puts us at risk. We may not know ahead of time what our consequences will be, but we must understand that they will come.

Do not be deceived, God is not mocked; for whatever a man sows, that he will also reap (Galatians 6:7).

It all comes down to the very basic spiritual law of sowing and reaping: you will reap what you sow. The seeds that you plant today will grow, mature, and eventually bear fruit in your future. This is a truth so self-evident that even the world has recognized it and assimilated it into their natural understanding of life.

If we consider this law in terms of our dreams, we will begin to understand the importance of each of the actions we take in pursuit of those dreams. Consider that every action you take, every decision you make while chasing your dream is essentially a seed that you are planting into your future. If the seeds that you plant are good (which is to say, if they are godly, righteous, honest, and just) then they will produce a good harvest – one that is filled with the power of a God-centered life. But when you plant seeds of dishonesty, sin, or even unrighteous attitudes like anger or unfor-giveness, you are setting yourself up to reap a harvest of calamity, negativity, failure, and even death.

The only safety that we have, the only guarantee that we are offered is that God's plan for our future us a good one, and filled with hope *(Jeremiah 29:11)*. His plan is to see our dreams come to pass. His hope for our future is that we will live in the fullness of all that He has placed in our hearts. But in order to receive this promise we must be willing to follow the plan – to walk, to act, and to speak in accordance with His guidance. We must plant seeds of life in order to reap the harvest that God most desires to give us.

Now it happened in the process of time that the king of Egypt died. Then the children of Israel groaned because of the bondage, and they cried out; and their cry came up to God because of the bondage (Exodus 2:23).

Moses' foolish sin sent him out of the country and into hiding. He was forced to flee for his life, and eventually found his way into a new existence in a land called Midian, where he became a shepherd. He married a local woman. And then ... well, nothing happened. He continued to live out an ordinary, average, unremarkable life as a shepherd in the desert. The man who had once been a prince of Egypt was stuck hiding in the wilderness for decades.

Moses lived in the desert doing nothing of consequence for a full forty years. In fact, the Bible tells us that it was only after the Pharaoh died that God was able to set back into motion His plan for the Israelite's deliverance. As long as that king of Egypt lived, Moses had a death sentence looming over his life. The potential consequences of his mistake were still waiting for him in Egypt, and their existence meant that everything Moses was born to do had to be put on hold.

You see, when we allow ourselves to fall into compromise and sin, we are not only hurting ourselves. It is not only our personal fulfillment that is delayed. We can never forget the larger picture, the greater impact that our dreams are supposed to have. Our dreams are meant to bless others, to redeem and restore the lives of countless individuals. Those are the people who suffer the most when we fail to walk in integrity. They are the ones who are stuck in bondage when our dreams are delayed.

But as important as it is for us to understand the consequences of trying to achieve our dreams our own way, it is equally important to realize that we should never give up hope. We will make mistakes along the way. We will disobey. We will make a mess of things. We are, after all, human. God knows this already, and in His infinite mercy, He has already offered us His forgiveness and redemption.

For the gifts and the calling of God are irrevocable. For as you were once disobedient to God, yet have now obtained mercy ... (Romans 11:29-30a).

This verse is so powerful, especially in the degree to which it applies to our pursuit of our dreams. Our mistakes will take us off track. They will set us back, and even put us on hold. But they cannot cause God to remove His gifts or His calling from our lives. We must, of course, strive for obedience. But even in our disobedience, the mercy of God is still there to fill our future with hope.

Moses committed murder – perhaps the most extreme act of sin that we as humans can imagine; and the consequences of his actions were severe. When his sin was discovered he was stripped of his rank, removed from power, and forced to flee the country. Even if he were able to go back to Egypt, he had lost all credibility both as an Egyptian ruler and as a spiritual leader among the Hebrews. By every natural measurement, any hope that he'd once had of setting the Israelites free was gone. The death of that one Egyptian man had effectively killed Moses' dream.

In God's eyes, however, the situation was far from hopeless. In fact, as far as the Lord was concerned Moses' dream was still very much alive. It didn't matter to God that he had essentially disqualified himself. It didn't matter to Him that even in the eyes of the world Moses was now unworthy of the task he'd once dreamed of completing. It didn't matter that he had essentially thrown away not only his dream, but his life in a single act of foolish aggression. As soon as the Pharaoh died, as soon as the natural obstacle to Moses' dream was removed, the Lord brought him right back to the beginning and revived the very dream that he had left for dead.

One day, as Moses was walking along, following after his sheep, he saw a bush that burned but was not consumed, and as he approached to take a closer look at it, the Lord began to speak:

"Now therefore, behold, the cry of the children of Israel has come to Me, and I have also seen the oppression with which the Egyptians oppress them. Come now, therefore, and I will send you to Pharaoh that you may bring My people, the children of Israel, out of Egypt"
(Exodus 3:9-10).

When God spoke to Moses from the burning bush, He did not rehash the sins of Moses' past. He didn't speak of his mistakes, or the price that he had been paying as a result of them. God simply told Moses that He wanted him to return to Egypt to deliver the people of Israel out of their bondage. After all those years, after what seemed like an absolute and final ending to Moses' dream, God confronted him and challenged him with a directive that seemed too good to be true.

God told Moses that He was sending him home to chase after his dream again.

But Moses said to God, "Who am I that I should go to Pharaoh, and that I should bring the children of Israel out of Egypt?" (Exodus 3:11)

I love Moses' reaction to God's command. He couldn't quite believe what the Lord was telling him. He actually asked God, "who am I?" Clearly, he had convinced himself that he was no longer qualified to do anything so meaningful. He didn't see how God could consider using him any longer. His dream, as far as he was concerned, was over.

It took a long time for God to convince Moses to go back and fulfill the destiny to which he'd been born. Moses used every excuse in the book. He didn't think the Israelites would believe that God sent him. He didn't see why they would bother listening to him. He didn't even consider himself capable of speaking on God's behalf. He certainly didn't see how he could speak with authority to the new Pharaoh. But the Lord wouldn't relent. He countered every objection, giving Moses every answer he could need, and even showed him how He would perform miracles on his behalf. There was nothing that Moses could say to convince God that He had picked the wrong man.

Finally, in an act of utter desperation, Moses resorted to begging, pleading with the Lord to send someone else, anyone else!

But he said, "O my Lord, please send by the hand of whomever else You may send" (Exodus 4:13).

God's answer, however, was unrelenting. He would not be moved. He would not give up on Moses. He would not allow him to remain in the wilderness of Midian any longer, not when there was a world-changing dream for him to chase back in Egypt.

You see, Moses had decided that he was disqualified, and as a result it seemed impossible that God would still be willing to use him. He knew how badly he had messed up – how could he not! He was living with the consequences every day. In fact, he had lived with those consequences for so many years that they seemed inescapable, a permanent and unchanging fact in his life.

Now the Lord said to Moses in Midian, "Go, return to Egypt; for all the men who sought your life are dead" (Exodus 4:19).

But in the Lord's eyes, all of that time that Moses spent in Midian, the time that seemed so final, so inescapable, was merely an inconvenient detour, a waiting period created by Moses' own actions. Yes, it would have been better if Moses had not sinned. Things may have moved quicker if he did not need to wait for his enemies to die. But once that problem was resolved, once the men who sought his life were dead, God was immediately ready to move Moses' dream forward.

Thank God that He refused to take Moses' *no* for an answer. Thank God that He pushed until Moses said *yes*! This was the moment when his life turned around and he was reunited with his future. He went back to Egypt, as God directed, and began the process of turning his dream into a reality.

This time, though, he made a point to speak and act in total obedience to the word of the Lord. Whatever God told him to do, he did – no matter how absurd or impossible it seemed. Whatever God told him to say, he said – even when it seemed insane. He did not act out of his own carnality any longer. He wasn't moved by emotions or circumstances. When no one agreed with him and everyone stood against him, Moses relied on the Lord. When the Pharaoh changed his mind and retracted his promises time and time again,

Moses refused to be moved. This time Moses pursued his dream according to God's pattern, and it wasn't long before he walked out of Egypt with the entire nation of Israel traveling behind him! His monumental and world-changing dream came to pass before his eyes. But it only happened when he decided that he was going to do things God's way, and not his own.

Even Jesus was faced with this same simple test. When He went into the wilderness after He was baptized, he encountered repeated temptations by Satan:

Again, the devil took Him up on an exceedingly high mountain, and showed Him all the kingdoms of the world and their glory. And he said to Him, "All these things I will give You if You will fall down and worship me"
(Mark 4:8-9).

The devil's final temptation was a simple one. He offered Jesus everything He wanted – all of the nations, all of the people that He had come to save. Satan was essentially offering Jesus a compromise, an "alternative" to the cross. He tried to convince God Himself that all He had to do to see His dream fulfilled was to fall down and worship him!

Now of course when we hear this bargain put in such blatant terms we find it horrifying and revolting. Who would ever choose to bow down and worship the devil just to get ahead? How could anyone believe that anything good would ever come of such an act? It's absolutely unthinkable. And yet, every time that we compromise, every time that we sin, every time that we sacrifice our spiritual integrity in pursuit of our dreams, this is the deal that we are making. We are essentially abandoning God's way in order to follow Satan. I think that we can all agree that we don't want to go down that road.

So ask yourself today: What choices am I making in order to see my dream fulfilled? Am I going places where I don't belong? Am I exposing myself to people or situations that will tempt me to sin? Am I lying, deceiving, hurting other people? Am I disobeying the law, engaging in immoral practices, cheating someone, or acting in disobedience to God's instructions? If your answer to any of these questions is yes, then this is your opportunity to change.

The lesson that we can take from Moses' story is a simple one. It starts with the understanding that you cannot disqualify yourself from your dreams. If God has given you a purpose in life then no one, not even you, can force Him to remove it. That dream, that purpose that you hold, it is yours no matter how badly you sin, no matter how big your mistakes may be. The passage of time is not proof of your failure. It does not mean that God has given up on you. In fact, you have no way of knowing how suddenly and how quickly He may move on your behalf to make your dream a reality.

That being said, we must understand that we are absolutely capable of removing ourselves from the path that God has set down for us to follow. When we act out of our own carnality or our human wisdom, when we choose to sin, to disobey God's laws, or to ignore His instructions, we will draw ourselves off course. This is dangerous, first because it removes us from the will of God, and second because it can have disastrous natural consequences that may be much larger than we could ever imagine! When we choose to do things our way as opposed to God's we are setting ourselves up for disappointments, problems, obstacles, and delays. It does not mean that our dreams are dead; but it does mean that we will need to take a longer, less direct, and more frustrating and painful path to realize them.

But this is not a mistake that we are required to make. We have the ability to choose God's way, right from the beginning. We have the ability to learn from Moses' actions, and to avoid his mistakes. So make the decision today to do things God's way no matter what. Decide that you will not be moved by circumstances, by emotions, by temptations, or by anything short of the will and direction of God. Choose to chase after your dream with integrity, no matter what other options may present themselves to you. It might not always make sense. It might, in fact, require immense amounts of faith and self control on your part. But rest assured, it is the quickest and most direct path to achieving your dreams.

BELIEVE

Caleb's Victorious Mindset

❖

We've just finished learning about how Moses' carnal choices delayed his journey towards the fulfillment of his dream. His life and his purpose were put on hold for years because, in his desire to see his people set free, he lashed out and killed one of their Egyptian oppressors. He had the purest and most godly of dreams, but because he reached for it in an ungodly way, his actions produced consequences that delayed his destiny. In this way, Moses' extreme example serves as a warning and a learning tool for each of us today.

But while it is important for us to understand how disastrous it is to deviate from from God's plan, it is equally important for us to realize that when it comes to our God given dreams, the time that passes and the obstacles we face are not signs of failure, and we should never use them as an excuse to give up.

Even Moses, who had every reason to believe that he had done irreparable damage to his own dream, was not able to remove himself from his destiny. It is true that he spent decades in the desert without any hint of progress. However, while the years of waiting that he endured in Midian may have been necessary, and while they were certainly a consequence of his own mistakes, they were not the end of his story. In fact, when that period of waiting was over, God completely transformed Moses' landscape and brought him right back to the path that he was meant to be traveling the whole time, as if nothing had gone wrong to begin with.

This leads us to another amazing revelation that we must embrace if we want to live productive and joy-filled lives while chasing after our dreams: we can never give up! There may be times when things won't go our way, times when we will come upon sudden obstacles, and times when we have to wait before we can reach for our dreams; but it is important for us to keep the right perspective as we go through these periods of opposition and waiting. We must not allow ourselves to surrender, to stop pressing forward, or to lose our zeal – even when the problems we face seem insurmountable, and even when the waiting periods feel impossibly long and difficult to endure.

Remember that God does not see our lives from the same limited, linear perspective as we do. It is so easy for us to see our present in infinite terms – as more real than the promises of our past and more powerful than the future towards which we are striving. But that is not how God operates. That's not how He plans. He knows our beginnings and our endings, He knows the peaks and the valleys that we will experience along the way, and through it all He is eternally faithful. He will bring us to the completion and realization of our dreams, if only we will follow after Him.

There may be times, even when you have done nothing wrong, when a problem will arise that you were not anticipating. Don't worry – that problem is not a surprise to God, and He has already provided a solution. Similarly, there may be times when you will be required to wait for the right season before you will be able to step into your destiny and to realize your dream. Sometimes they are not even seasons of your own making. They may, in fact, be the result of circumstances that are completely beyond your control. Those times, however, are not a surprise to God either. He has not forgotten or abandoned you in those desolate places. If He led you into them, He will lead you out as well.

There is one man in the Bible who lived in absolute certainty of this truth, even though it took him a lifetime to reach his dream. This man's name was Caleb.

Caleb was a man of incredible faith and unwavering passion. He was fearless in the face of adversity because he understood that God was the one who would lead him into his dream. However, circumstances beyond his control put his dream out of reach not just for years, but for decades.

Nevertheless, when his opportunity finally came, he did not hesitate for a moment before claiming what was his. He wasn't plagued with doubts or fears. The passage of time had done nothing to dampen his zeal, and even in his old age he was aggressive in his pursuit of the dream before him.

When the Bible first introduces us to Caleb, it is in the midst of a turbulent point in Israel's history. Moses had recently led the entire Hebrew nation out of Egypt and into the wilderness. They all willingly followed him, not only because he was releasing them from slavery, but because he told them that God was leading them into a land of their own. After spending some time traveling through the desert, they had finally arrived at the borders of Canaan, the very land that God had promised to Abraham, their forefather.

And the Lord spoke to Moses, saying, "Send men to spy out the land of Canaan, which I am giving to the children of Israel; from each tribe of their fathers you shall send a man, every one a leader among them"
(Numbers 13:1-2).

God instructed Abraham to send spies into Canaan, and He specifically explained that this was the land He intended to give to the Israelites as their inheritance. Moses obeyed God's instructions, selecting a leader from each tribe to go into the land as spies, including Caleb, a leader of the tribe of Judah *(Numbers 13:6).* It is important to realize that these men were not selected at random. They were hand-picked for their respectability, for their leadership qualities, and for their trustworthiness. Moses selected men that the people would listen to, just as God instructed, and he sent them into Canaan to survey the land and report what they'd found.

Then they told him, and said: "We went to the land where you sent us. It truly flows with milk and honey, and this is its fruit. Nevertheless the people who dwell in the land are strong; the cities are fortified and very large; moreover we saw the descendants of Anak there"
(Numbers 13:27-28).

When the spies returned from their mission, they came bearing both good and bad news. On the one hand, they saw that their dream – their promised land – was every bit as wonderful as God had said it would be. It was rich and fertile, a land flowing with milk and honey, full of every good and beautiful fruit. It was a virtual paradise in comparison with the harsh conditions that they had lived under for so long. Suddenly their dream had taken on physical form. They had seen it with their own eyes. It existed, it was within reach, and it was wonderful to behold.

But together with that amazing news, they'd discovered a problem that they weren't prepared to face: the dream that they were chasing had already been taken. The land that God had promised them was already inhabited by powerful nations who had built fortified cities. Some of them were even descendants of a race of giants! To a ragtag group of former slaves, this must have been a truly imposing prospect.

Clearly the spies were not expecting to find this kind of barrier standing between them and the fulfillment of their dream. I'm sure that as they first went out to examine the land, they hoped that they would find it unpopulated, or at least filled with the type of people that could be easily conquered. After all, God had told them that this land would be theirs. So to suddenly discover a powerful enemy blocking their way at the very threshold of their promise was startling and worrying.

However, among the spies who returned, there was one who was not particularly concerned with the size of their enemies. This man had a truly God-centered perspective on the situation:

Then Caleb quieted the people before Moses, and said, "Let us go up at once and take possession, for we are well able to overcome it" (Numbers 13:30).

Caleb, the spy from Judah, was quick to tell the people that their dream was still possible. He was not worried about the giants in the land. He was not focused on how insurmountable the barriers to their success appeared. He refused to let the issues define his chances of success. Instead, his focus was on the Lord, and on the incredible power that comes when a people are willing to chase after God's plan.

Caleb was a man of passion and zeal. He saw the land of Canaan as ready for the taking, and he was eager to help his people move forward into their destinies. He was not willing to consider delay, not when he had seen the blessing with his own eyes. He had an incredible understanding – that if God had promised this land to him, then that meant it was already his.

Remember that the Israelites had just experienced a season of miracles unlike anything we can even begin to imagine. With their own eyes they witnessed the ten plagues that ravaged the land of Egypt. They all walked through the Red Sea on dry ground, and then watched as it closed behind them and swallowed their enemies. They had spent their time in the wilderness following after a pillar that looked like a cloud in the daytime and fire at night. They had seen water pour from rocks and eaten bread that fell each morning from heaven.

Is it really any wonder, then, that Caleb was so confident in his faith? Is it really all that surprising that he was unphased, even by the literal giants that he found waiting on the other side of the river? Given all that he had witnessed, why would he worry, even for a moment, that these Canaanites could stop him from claiming what the Almighty God of Heaven had offered to him?

But the men who had gone up with him said, "We are not able to go up against the people, for they are stronger than we." And they gave the children of Israel a bad report of the land which they had spied out" (Numbers 13:31-32a).

Unfortunately, the other spies who came back from Canaan did not share Caleb's perspective. In their eyes, their adversaries were so frightening that the very idea of attempting to stand against them seemed like a death-wish. They argued that the giants were stronger, as if that was what really mattered. They'd completely lost sight of the fact that their enemy's strength was nothing in comparison with the power of God. When they looked with their natural eyes and saw their natural enemies it sparked such fear in them that they forgot they weren't limited by the natural world. They forgot they were a supernatural people!

These spies made a simple mistake. They allowed themselves to become so focused on their comparative weakness that they completely lost sight of the power that was prepared to propel them forward and crush any enemy that tried to stand against them. It was as if seeing giants with their own eyes caused them to forget everything that God had done for them up until that very moment. They weren't even able to take into consideration the fact that it was God who had sent them to spy out the land in the first place.

As a result, they let their fear steal any zeal that they may have had, and they gave the people a bad report. Essentially, they told the Israelites that there was no point in trying to claim the land, because as far as they were able to see, they were doomed to fail.

Imagine that! Imagine walking out of slavery, crossing a desert, coming to the border of the very land your people have dreamed of possessing for 400 years, and hearing that it was all for nothing! I cannot begin to think of a more disheartening moment, a more crushing disappointment. It almost makes the Israelites' reaction seem perfectly rational:

And all the children of Israel complained against Moses and Aaron, and the whole congregation said to them, "If only we had died in the land of Egypt! Or if only we had died in this wilderness! Why has the Lord brought us to this land to fall by the sword, that our wives and children should become victims? Would it not be better for us to return to Egypt?" So they said to one another, "Let us select a leader and return to Egypt" (Numbers 14:2-4).

The people's reaction to the apparent impossibility of their dream was a simple one: they turned themselves into victims. Because they could not see a way out, they determined that there was no way out. Because the opposition seemed too strong, they assumed that they would be defeated. Because they could not see God's hand making the way for them, they believed that He had abandoned them to death. Faced with an enemy they weren't expecting to find, they wanted to give up, to stop chasing their dream, and to go back to their bondage.

Don't judge these people too harshly, though, because many people still make this same mistake today. It can be so easy start off moving towards our dreams with great expectations, believing that God is taking us into a beautiful future. When things are going our way and we see God's hand guiding us, it takes very little effort to move forward in faith. But how do we react when that ever-present hand leads us somewhere a little less pleasant? What is our response when we encounter a challenge or an obstacle that we didn't see coming? Suddenly, facing unexpected fears and unforeseen problems, it can become very easy to second guess our once-solid assurance. We can be just as quick as the Israelites to interpret any serious opposition as a sign of God's abandonment. And just like the Israelites, we can quickly lose our nerve and look for a way to retrace our steps.

But Joshua the son of Nun and Caleb the son of Jephunneh, who were among those who had spied out the land, tore their clothes; and they spoke to all the congregation of the children of Israel, saying: "The land we passed through to spy out is an exceedingly good land. If the Lord delights in us, then He will bring us into this land and give it to us, 'a land which flows with milk and honey'" (Numbers 14:6-8).

Amazingly, not all of the Israelites were swayed by the impossibility of the dream that they were chasing. Two men, Joshua and Caleb, were willing to imagine that the God who had promised them this land was powerful enough to actually give it to them, despite the seemingly insurmountable odds that they faced. They understood that the battle was not won by the strongest army or the most powerful people. They saw that it was the favor of the Lord that really mattered. If His hand was with them, they couldn't see how it would be possible to fail.

In fact, when they saw that the Israelites were getting ready to return to Egypt they were so horrified that they tore their clothes. They understood that they were one small step away from their destiny. They were literally on the threshold of receiving their promises. The idea of allowing the people to walk away from it all must have been absolutely unthinkable; and so they did everything in their power to convince their countrymen not to give up on their dreams.

Nevertheless, the people would not be persuaded. Their minds had been so overcome by the negative reports of the other ten spies that traveling into Canaan was no longer an option. They became convinced that their dream was impossible, and so they turned their backs on the promises of God. They were so sure of their own failure that they became unwilling to even try.

Isn't it amazing how effective negative words can be in persuading someone to let go of their dreams? Sometimes all it takes is an expert, a doctor, or a trusted confidant saying, "that's impossible," to send a person off of the path onto which God has placed them. All it took in the case of the Israelites was the opinion of a few well-respected leaders.

We must be wary of the negative voices that will try to dissuade us from our God given purposes. If you have a dream, you can rest assured that there will be people who will tell you that it is impossible. There will be those who will sincerely attempt to warn you of the dangers and obstacles that stand in your path. These words won't be spoken randomly – there will be very real and legitimate reasons for saying them. In fact, you will often hear completely rational and logical arguments to explain why your dream can't happen. After all, if it was easy to achieve, it really wouldn't be much of dream would it? But just because the arguments are rational does not mean that we should be listening to them.

It is important for us to keep our minds firmly fixed on the one thing that these Israelites forgot: if God is the One who gave us our dreams, then He is the One who will empower us to achieve them. Do not let the natural arguments or persuasions of mere men stop you from seeing the larger picture drawn by your Almighty Savior. Do not forget that you serve a God who raises people from the dead, splits oceans in half, heals incurable diseases, and sends armies fleeing from before His people. No matter how big your dream, no matter how insurmountable the obstacle, and no matter how impossible the circumstances, nothing – *absolutely nothing* – is impossible with God *(Luke 1:37)*.

Make no mistake, there will be people in your life who will speak negative words about your dreams, just like the ten spies did when they spoke to the Israelites. Many of them will do it in all sincerity of heart and with the best of intentions. They will be people you know well, even people you trust. Some will have the authority and expertise to command your respect. Most of them will not be looking to actively crush your dreams. However, the words that they speak will have the power to influence your perspective, and the potential to draw you away from the truth that God has planted in your heart.

Your reaction to these negative voices is of vital importance, because it has the power to establish your future. Determine now that you will not allow them to sway you. Decide in your heart that you will refuse to become a victim of circumstance. Make the choice now that you will never stop chasing after you dreams, no matter what. Do that, and God will lead you into your victory.

However, when you give those negative voices the ability to hold sway over your thoughts, you will put yourself in a dangerous position: the very position that the Israelites found themselves in at this point in their journey. They allowed the voices of men to persuade them that their God-given dream was impossible, and because of that they refused to move forward. They refused to follow where He was taking them. They made it impossible for Him to lead them into their promised land, and as a result, every single one of them missed out on their blessing:

"because all these men who have seen My glory and the signs which I did in Egypt and in the wilderness, and have put Me to the test now these ten times, and have not heeded My voice, they certainly shall not see the land of which I swore to their fathers, nor shall any of those who rejected Me see it. But My servant Caleb, because he has a different spirit in him and has followed Me fully, I will bring into the land where he went, and his descendants shall inherit it" (Numbers 14:22-24).

Even in this moment, God still fully intended to honor his promise to His people. The nation of Israel was still going to receive their dream. But that dream could no longer be realized by the people that He had taken out of Egypt. As much as He wanted them to walk into Canaan in that moment and claim their victory (that was His plan, remember) the people themselves refused to move forward.

God wasn't able to use a people who refused to trust in His ability to fight their battles for them. How could He? If they were unwilling to even attempt to go where He sent them, how could He possibly lead them into their dream? The simple answer is that He couldn't. Their disobedience tied His hands, and as a result the promise that God had intended for that moment was delayed for an entire generation.

It is heartbreaking to consider that an entire nation of people allowed themselves to be talked out of a dream that was on the verge of becoming reality. They gave the words of a handful of influential men more sway, more weight, than the promise and instructions of the Lord. They allowed negative voices to convince them of their own victimhood – and they lived out the rest of their lives in exactly that state.

God did not abandon these people. He took care of them. He provided for them and fed them. He kept their sandals from wearing out and their clothes from disintegrating. But they never walked into their promised land.

In fact, out of the entire nation of Israel, there were only two men, Joshua and Caleb, who believed that their dream was possible to achieve. God took note of their faith, and He said that those two men would be the only ones out of their generation to cross over the Jordan and see the land that they had been promised.

It was forty years before God led the Israelites back to the river Jordan, back to the border of their blessing. By that time every single man who had stood there the first time was dead, except for Joshua and Caleb, the two spies that had embraced their God-given dreams with zeal.

Just as the Lord had said, He led the next generation of Israelites across the river and into their promises. The giants of the land were still there forty years later. The circumstances hadn't actually changed. The enemy was still as formidable as ever. Even the cities still stood. But this time, led by Joshua, the people of Israel marched across the Jordan as victors, ready to claim the dream that had been promised to their fathers.

Perhaps the most incredible thing about this story is that when they were obedient, when they walked into their God-given inheritance the Israelites discovered that their enemies (the same ones who had seemed so impossibly large to their fathers) were trembling in fear at their approach. In fact, when Joshua sent men to spy out the land, just as Moses had done forty years earlier, they infiltrated the city of Jericho and discovered that all of the people were living in fear because they'd heard that Israel was on its way.

"I know that the Lord has given you the land, that the terror of you has fallen on us, and that all the inhabitants of the land are fainthearted because of you ... And as soon as we heard these things, our hearts melted; neither did there remain any more courage in anyone because of you, for the Lord your God, He is God in heaven above and on earth beneath" (Judges 2:9, 11).

Imagine that. Imagine being one of those spies and discovering that the entire city of Jericho was terrified to hear that your people were about to enter their territory. Imagine realizing that the very giants whom your fathers had run from were deathly afraid because they'd heard that you were on their doorstep. Imagine seeing that even this city full of godless idol worshippers could recognize that you would not be fighting the battles by yourselves. Imagine hearing your enemies proclaiming that the Lord God had given their land to you, and that there would be no people, no city, no army that could stand against His might!

I would guess that those spies returned to Joshua and the people with a much better report than the ten men Moses had sent a generation earlier. Even though the land was the same, even though the enemy was the same, their perspective would have been completely different. These men could not see themselves as victims, no matter how large or imposing their enemies may have seemed. They had heard confirmation from the mouths of the very people who stood in their way that God was on their side. They understood, as their fathers had not, that even before the battles had been fought they were already victorious.

In fact, God was so determined to see His people claim their dreams that even the walls of the city could not stand before His will. When the Israelites marched around Jericho according to His instruction, the Lord literally knocked the city walls down flat before them. From there, they went on to demolish one army after another, defeating kings, cities, and entire nations of people. No one was capable of standing against them. Nothing could block their way. The land, the dream was theirs, and they were seeing the realization of God's promise manifest before their very eyes.

It was in the midst of this great victory march that Caleb, now an old man, came before Joshua to speak to him about the dream that they'd shared for so long:

*Then the children of Judah came to Joshua in Gilgal.
And Caleb the son of Jephunneh the Kenizzite said to him:
"You know the word which the Lord said to Moses the man
of God concerning you and me in Kadesh Barnea. I was
forty years old when Moses the servant of the Lord sent me
from Kadesh Barnea to spy out the land, and I brought
back word to him as it was in my heart"* (Joshua 14:6-7).

Oh how I love this phrase that Caleb used: *"I brought
back word to him as it was in my heart."* To me this speaks
volumes about Caleb's character, about his perspective.
When he first spoke to Moses and to the people, he wasn't
speaking from a place of practicality. He wasn't being
rational. He was speaking words from his heart. He was
speaking in faith, and more importantly he was ready to put
that faith into action!

If it were up to Caleb there would have been no
decades-long waiting period. There probably wouldn't have
even been a discussion. If Caleb had his way, the entire
nation of Israel would have jumped at that first opportunity
they'd been given, marched across the Jordan river, and
taken the land without a second thought.

*"Nevertheless my brethren who went up with me
made the heart of the people melt, but I wholly followed the
Lord my God. So Moses swore on that day, saying, 'Surely
the land where your foot has trodden shall be your
inheritance and your children's forever, because you have
wholly followed the Lord my God'"* (Joshua 14:8-9).

What's amazing about these words is that they show us
how little Caleb's perspective had changed over the course

of those long years. He was not focused on the passage of time that he had been forced to endure. His eyes were not on the many men who had died during the time of waiting. He was not bitter, cynical, angry, or afraid. What Caleb remembered was the promise that God had made to him – the promise that he would enter into Canaan and claim the land that he had walked over as a spy.

Caleb did not allow anything to take his eyes off of his dream. He would not be swayed, distracted, or defeated, not even by years of wandering in circles through the desert. He had grabbed hold of a promise, and there was nothing that could make him let go.

"And now, behold, the Lord has kept me alive, as He said, these forty-five years, ever since the Lord spoke this word to Moses while Israel wandered in the wilderness; and now, here I am this day, eighty-five years old. As yet I am as strong this day as on the day that Moses sent me; just as my strength was then, so now is my strength for war, both for going out and for coming in. Now therefore, give me this mountain of which the Lord spoke in that day" (Joshua 14:10-12a).

How incredible is this speech that Caleb made? At eighty five years old, after waiting more than half of his lifetime to walk into dream, he was not only prepared to fight for his inheritance – he was eager to get started! Time had not lessened his zeal. As far as he was concerned, it hadn't even affected his strength. His moment had come again. His dream was within his reach. He was just as bold and confident about his ability to claim it at the age of eighty five as he had been at forty.

Caleb went on to capture the city of Hebron and win the very land that he had walked over as a spy forty five years earlier. He and his family received all that God had promised to them. His dream was realized, and he was there to see it happen.

The secret to Caleb's success wasn't luck. It wasn't strength or longevity or even endurance. He was victorious for the same reason that the entire nation of Israel was victorious. His victory came from his unwavering belief that God was going to give him what He'd promised. No matter how long he had to wait, no matter what obstacles he faced, no matter how old he got, Caleb never took his eyes off of his dream. He never gave up, never allowed himself to become a victim. Throughout the ups and downs, the disappointments and the delays, he kept his zeal sharp. No wonder he was so well prepared to claim what God was offering him!

The dreams that God has placed in our hearts are there for a reason. They are there because He intends for us to receive them, to claim them, and to walk in them. But as in every part of our lives, we have decisions to make about how we will approach these dreams.

We can choose to walk a natural path, making our decisions based on the circumstances and situations that we can see with our eyes. We can allow our emotions to be swayed with every problem, every obstacle that happens to impede our progress. We can do what the first generation of

Israelites did, and allow others to convince us that our dreams are impossible to reach, that the cost is too high.

Or we can choose to walk the path of faith. We can choose to put our eyes not on our natural circumstances but on the hand of God that is leading us onward. We can choose to listen not to the voices of fear and doubt, but to the command of our Lord, following His direction and obeying His instruction. We can choose to trust not in our own natural understanding or our human capacity to judge a situation, but in the supernatural strength of the Lord.

When we choose the second way, we will find ourselves living the life of a victor and not a victim. When our eyes are on God and the dreams that He is offering us, it will not matter what our circumstances look like any more. It won't matter what others are saying, or what giants stand in our path. The passage of time will no longer seem like a sign of our own stagnation or failure, but instead as a measure of our constant progress towards the day when our dreams will be realized.

So choose today – choose to be a Caleb. Decide now that your eyes will be on the Lord, that your confidence is in Him, and that you are following His plan no matter what. Make the quality decision that you will find your victory now, before you even face your battles. If you do, you will discover that there is nothing that can quench your zeal.

PREPARE

DAVID'S WORK ETHIC

❖❖

In preparation for this book, I spent some time speaking to people about their dreams, their deepest desires. Do you know what I discovered? Most of the people I spoke to believed that their dreams were completely achievable. Some of them said that the things that they were dreaming of would be difficult to attain, but overall they were not dreaming for things that they considered impossible. Their dreams were for things that seemed within their grasp.

The amazing thing, however, was that while an overwhelming majority of people believed that their dreams were achievable, less than half of them claimed to be regularly and actively preparing for the day when those dreams would come true. Fewer still had a plan of action to help them get there!

That one basic fact, that fundamental difference between what people dream of for their futures and what they do in their present, spoke volumes to me about why so many fail to see their dreams become a reality. After all, we cannot reasonably expect to arrive at a destination if we are not willing to make the effort to travel there. We cannot expect to achieve a goal tomorrow that we are not working towards today. And yet, that is exactly what so many dreamers do. They look into their future and imagine it filled with their hearts' desires. But because they see those dreams as a part of some distant "tomorrow" they fail to do the things in the present that will help get them there. That simple disconnect, that basic lack of understanding, robs them of their futures!

This brings us to the fourth fundamental principle that we must learn about in our quest to become active dream chasers. If we are serious about achieving our dreams tomorrow then we should be doing everything in our power to prepare for them today. This is simple and practical advice. It is so simple, in fact, that many people have no problem accepting it as true and completely ignoring it at the same time. But the implications of this basic principle are too important for us to ignore any longer.

We serve a sudden and miraculous God who will often open unexpected doors in order to lead us directly into our destinies. We cannot always know or even imagine when or how our dreams will come to pass. As often as not, they overtake us in the most surprising ways and at the most unexpected times. Knowing this, we must recognize our own responsibility to prepare ourselves for that moment now. We must be willing to take positive and decisive action in order to make ourselves ready for the day when our dreams will arrive.

Ask yourself: if my dream came true tomorrow, if it suddenly fell into my lap, would I be ready to take full advantage of it? Am I as equipped, trained, educated, and prepared as I will need to be when that moment comes? If the answer to either of these questions is no, then the next question you need to ask yourself is this: what is holding me back?

It is time for us to take ownership of the role we are supposed to play in making our dreams a reality. We have a responsibility to prepare ourselves for the things that we desire to achieve. Whether your dream is something that you can reach on your own, or something so large that it would take a miracle to see it accomplished, there is room for you to begin preparing for it now.

Maybe there are skills that you can sharpen or talents that you can develop while you're waiting on your dream. Maybe you can take advantage of the time you have now to further your education, or to learn more about the specific industry or career path that you dream of entering. Maybe there is a piece of your personality or a facet of your character that God wants you to work on changing before He places you in the position or relationship that you're dreaming of. Do not despise these small beginnings, these basic acts of preparation. They may be mundane, difficult, or time-consuming; but when God opens the door to your dream (whether it happens tomorrow or ten years from now) you will find that these small, ordinary tasks have shaped and molded you into exactly the person you will need to be.

There is a wonderful example of this level of practical preparation in the Bible, in the story of King David. Now most of us know David as the young shepherd who defeated Goliath and eventually became the second king to rule over Israel. But David was so much more than that. He was a psalmist, a musician, and a true worshipper. The Bible tells us that he was a man after God's own heart (*1 Samuel 13:14*). In other words, he had an authentic and deep relationship with the Lord.

It should come as no surprise, then, that David didn't have big dreams of extending his influence, defeating his enemies, or increasing his power. In fact, he didn't dream of anything for himself at all. His dream was to build a temple – a permanent house in which God's presence could dwell among the people:

Now it came to pass when the king was dwelling in his house, and the Lord had given him rest from all his enemies all around, that the king said to Nathan the prophet, "See now, I dwell in a house of cedar, but the ark of God dwells inside tent curtains" (2 Samuel 7:1-2).

After David was done fighting his wars, he looked around and took stock of his life. He saw the beautiful house that he lived in, the power that he wielded as king, and the comfort and prestige that came with his position. His reaction to all that he had been given was so amazing – he wanted to give that same glory, that same prestige, that same honor back to God. He decided that he wanted to build God's temple.

David's dream was beautiful and righteous. It was an honorable and noble desire, but he had a problem. When David shared all that was in his heart, God sent a prophet to tell him not to do it.

Then King David rose to his feet and said, "Hear me, my brethren and my people: I had it in my heart to build a house of rest for the ark of the covenant of the Lord, and for the footstool of our God, and had made preparations to build it. But God said to me, 'You shall not build a house for My name, because you have been a man of war and have shed blood' (1 Chronicles 28: 2-3).

The Lord could not allow David to build His house, because although David's heart was pure and righteous before the God, his life had been filled with war and death. He had too much blood on his hands, and it was not proper for a king with such a violent legacy to be the one who built the temple of the Lord.

Now, at first glance this may seem like a terrible turn of events in David's life. After all God had effectively shut the door on his dream. He told David that he would never be allowed to fulfill his own heart's desire, even though it was completely within his power to do so. However, this was not the end of David's story. In fact, as He so often does, God extended David's dream, expanding it to heights that he had not even asked for:

"When your days are fulfilled and you rest with your fathers, I will set up your seed after you, who will come from your body, and I will establish his kingdom. He shall build a house for My name, and I will establish the throne of his kingdom forever (2 Samuel 7:12-13).

God could not allow David to build His temple, so instead He gave him something even better. He made a covenant with David. He told David that it would be his son, Solomon, who would become king after him and build the temple of the Lord. Furthermore, God promised that there would be a king from David's line sitting on the throne of Israel forever. In fact, in fulfillment of that promise, Jesus Christ himself was born in the lineage of David!

Because David wanted to build God's house, God blessed him by establishing his own house, his own lineage into future generations. Because David was willing to give his dream to God, the Lord was able to expand it until it became a blessing that touched more than just the nation of Israel. It became the vehicle by which salvation was extended to all of us, Jew and Gentile alike. David's dream started off as something beautiful, something that would bring glory to God; but the Lord changed it and transformed it until it became something powerful enough to alter history.

All of that was very lovely and incredibly powerful – but in the end it still left David in the position of being unable to see his own dream through to completion. Nevertheless, even in this moment of disappointment, David had the right attitude. He recognized that even though he would not be the one to build the temple, that did not mean that he was powerless to contribute to its ultimate success. The honor of the final achievement may have been passed to his son, but David saw that there was still so much that he could do to ensure that his dream would become a reality.

Now David said, "Solomon my son is young and inexperienced, and the house to be built for the Lord must be exceedingly magnificent, famous and glorious through-out all countries. I will now make preparation for it." So David made abundant preparations before his death
(1 Chronicles 22:5).

David decided long before his son started to build the temple that he was going to do everything in his power to make sure Solomon succeeded. He was determined that God's temple would be absolutely glorious; and even though his dream would not be fulfilled in his lifetime, he saw that there was work that he could do immediately to pave the way for its eventual completion. So from that moment forward, David began to make preparations for the temple. Isn't that such a powerful example for us to follow?

David's made the decision that he would be active in pursuing his dream, even though he knew that dream was being passed down to his son. He made sure that he was obedient to the Lord's instructions – he didn't presume to attempt to build the temple himself. But he did not give up on it either. Instead he began to plan, to gather resources, and to make all of the preparations that would be necessary so that when the temple was eventually built it would be a magnificent success.

This, of course, leads us back to the question that we asked at the beginning of this chapter; namely, how much effort are you putting into preparations for your own dream right now?

It can be very easy to put our dreams off to the side, to leave them unattended while we go about our daily lives. This is especially true when those dreams seem far off or when things aren't progressing in the way that we would like. But these dreams are ours for a reason. God has given them to us for a purpose. So even if we are not in a position to claim our dreams today, that should never stop us from doing all that is in our power to prepare for them while we wait.

This all circles back to the concept of waiting. You may face times of delay, times when it is impossible to actively pursue the dreams that are in your heart. However, you must be very careful in those times of waiting to differentiate between forward progress (which may not be possible) and preparation (which almost always is).

Waiting does not have to be a passive activity. In fact, those days, months, or years that you spend waiting for you dream can be some of the most productive and valuable times of your life! Don't sit idly back simply because your dream is not available at this moment. Don't neglect the desires that God has put into your heart just because you don't see their fulfillment on your immediate horizon. Take advantage of the time that you have been given, and begin to prepare yourself for the day that your dream does come.

Your dreams belong to God, but He has given them to you to achieve. If you are invested in seeing them come to pass, then the best thing that you can do is to behave like you know that they're coming. Act now as though you sincerely believe that God is going to give you your dreams tomorrow. Order your priorities, set aside your time, and make your preparations as if your dreams were already in front of you. When you do this, you will not only be laying a practical foundation for your future, but you will also be exercising your faith.

Thus also faith by itself, if it does not have works, is dead. But someone will say, "You have faith, and I have works." Show me your faith without your works, and I will show you my faith by my works (James 2:17-18).

This is a very well known scripture, but I believe that it is often misunderstood, or at least too narrowly applied. We understand these verses to mean that if we are sincere in our faith, then our actions will reflect that sincerity. However, many people limit the application of this truth to things that they see as "spiritual" and completely neglect the impact that it should have on their practical life decisions.

We need to understand, however, that faith is a very practical thing. It is more than just believing that God's promises are true. It means believing that those promises are true right now – even if their fulfillment hasn't come and won't come for some time. In Hebrews 11, for example, the Bible speaks of person after person who made decisions and acted upon them based on the understanding that God's promises were more true than their present situations. God's word bore more weight in their *today* decisions than their immediate present circumstances. Because they believed in the future that God was offering them more than they believed in the present circumstances they saw all around them they made decisions based on that future and not the present – and those decisions were therefore made by faith.

Can you see how great an impact this understanding of faith will have on your pursuit of your dreams? If your present tells you that you're just another ordinary failure, and that your dreams are impossible, but you are believing God that He is going to fulfill the dream that He's given you, then you have a choice to make. In every moment, in every situation, you can choose to act as if you are either a failure or a success, ordinary or extraordinary. You can choose to behave as if your dream is attainable or as if it is not. If you believe in God's promise for your future as if it is His promise for your present – if you believe that you are an extraordinary success now more than you believe that you're an ordinary failure, then you'll begin to make choices that reflect that faith.

That is what David did when he decided to prepare for the temple. His circumstances looked like failure, but he did not let them stop him. He did not care that God's promises felt far off – he decided to act on them anyway. He spent the rest of his life proactively demonstrating his faith in God by doing all that was in his power to prepare for the day that his dream would become a reality.

So David commanded to gather the aliens who were in the land of Israel; and he appointed masons to cut hewn stones to build the house of God. And David prepared iron in abundance for the nails of the doors of the gates and for the joints, and bronze in abundance beyond measure, and cedar trees in abundance; (1 Chronicles 22:2-4a)

This verse contains such an important lesson that it deserves the time that it will take for us to delve a little deeper into it. You see, it can be so easy to assume that David started off on this endeavor with a grand master-plan already in place. But the only thing that the Bible actually tells us is that he had a dream. In fact, we have no real reason to assume that David had the slightest clue about to how to go about building a temple. He had grown up a shepherd, and spent his adulthood as a warrior. What did he know about constructing even the simplest of buildings, let alone something as majestic and ambitious as the temple of the Lord?

So when he decided that he was going to dedicate the rest of his life to making preparations for this magnificent temple to honor his God, I imagine that he may have felt just the tiniest bit out of his element. I know I would have! In fact, if I were in his position, I probably wouldn't even have known where to start.

But David was a determined man. He wasn't going to let a little thing like inexperience stop him. So how did he begin planning and preparing to build? He started with the basics – wood and stone, iron and bronze.

David looked at the monumental task that stood before him, and he started with the things that he could work on immediately. He may not have known much about temple-building, but he knew that it would have to be built of stone; and so he began the work of quarrying and cutting stones. He knew that there would be doors and paneling, and so he started collecting wood. Those doors would need hinges, and the building would obviously need nails too, so he gathered iron as well. He began with the fundamentals, and allowed the process of preparation to grow and expand from there.

This is encouraging news – especially for those of us whose dreams do not fit neatly within the range of our current areas of expertise. If you are attempting to prepare for a dream that feels larger than life, or one that takes you outside of your comfort zone, just do what David did. If the whole thing seems to large, too complex, or too intricate to figure out, then let yourself start at the beginning. It's ok if you don't know exactly what you're doing. It's ok if the amount of skill, work, resources, or knowledge that your dream requires seems beyond your ability. Don't let the magnitude of your task unnerve you.

If you're ready to begin preparing for a dream but you don't know where to start, begin with the simplest thing. Find a basic task, one that is easy to do, one that you know needs to be done, and begin doing it. Then do the next thing that comes to hand, and then the next. You will be surprised at how easily those small, simple tasks feed into larger, more complex ones, and at how quickly you can begin to conquer that insurmountable pile of work.

This is exactly what David did, and his results speak for themselves:

Then David gave his son Solomon the plans for the vestibule, its houses, its treasuries, its upper chambers, its inner chambers, and the place of the mercy seat; and the plans for all that he had by the Spirit, of the courts of the house of the Lord, of all the chambers all around, of the treasuries of the house of God, and of the treasuries for the dedicated things; also for the division of the priests and the Levites, for all the work of the service of the house of the Lord, and for all the articles of service in the house of the Lord (1 Chronicles 28:11-13).

By the time David reached the end of his life, he had moved well beyond collecting iron and wood. What had started off with a few simple slabs of stone had grown into the immeasurable mountain of material that it would take to see the temple built.

As the years went by and his preparations became more involved, David actually went so far as to write down detailed plans for every aspect of the temple he wanted his son to build. These were more than thumbnail sketches. They were intricate and precise blueprints. He may not have started off with more than the vaguest notion of what the temple would look like, but by the end he knew exactly how many chambers he wanted built and where they should be. He knew the sizes and the placements of each of the vestibules and the treasuries. He even wrote up a work schedule for the priests and Levites who would be ministering there. In other words – David had done some serious planning!

As a result, David was able to complete his preparations with extraordinary precision. He no longer had to guess how much iron or wood he would need. He did not have to estimate the weight of gold that would be required to cover the walls or how much room should be set aside for treasuries. Every facet of this project was thought through and calculated in painstaking detail.

He was therefore completely confident that he was equipping his son with everything he could possibly need in order to build the temple. He not only gave him a treasure-trove of riches and resources, but also a step by step plan of action to transform them into a house worthy of God's glory.

Furthermore King David said to all the assembly: "My son Solomon, whom alone God has chosen, is young and inexperienced; and the work is great, because the temple is not for man but for the Lord God. Now for the house of my God I have prepared with all my might: gold for things to be made of gold, silver for things of silver, bronze for things of bronze, iron for things of iron, wood for things of wood, onyx stones, stones to be set, glistening stones of various colors, all kinds of precious stones, and marble slabs in abundance (1 Chronicles 29:1-2).

When it came time for David to pass his dream on to his son, he called together the leaders and rulers of his land to bear witness to what was happening. As he presented his dream to these men, the one thing that stood out immediately was the sheer dedication that he had put into the work. He had committed years of his life to making sure that every detail was in absolute readiness. In fact, he told the people that he had literally prepared with all of his might.

Nothing was beneath his notice, because every detail contributed to the overall success of the dream that was burning in his heart. Every nail, every tile, every precious stone that he'd collected was a piece of a larger picture, a part of a greater whole. I would imagine that over the years as David lovingly counted, weighed, and measured each bar of bronze, each plank of wood, that he spent time picturing where each piece might fit and what purpose it might serve.

Of course this holds a very simple and practical lesson for us as well: if we are going to take the time and the effort to prepare for our dreams, it is worth our while to do it correctly. Don't allow the little details to escape your notice. The dream that you have is worthy of your time. It's worthy of your effort. It's worth the work, worth the research, and worth the resources that you will need to put into it. However, it bears repeating that all of this precision, this incredible level of detail was only possible because David had a written plan.

Plans, blueprints, and instructions are very important to God. We can find examples of this all through the Bible. In the book of Habakkuk, God spoke to His prophet and gave him instructions to write down the vision that he had been given *(Habakkuk 2:2)*. Moses spent forty days on a mountaintop while God give him explicit written blueprints for the first tabernacle that was built *(see Exodus 24-32)*. Likewise, when David presented his plans for his dream of the temple, the Bible tells us that they were inspired by the Spirit *(1 Chronicles 28:12)*. If God wrote down His plan for Moses, instructed Habakkuk to write down his vision, and inspired David put his plans on paper as well, is there any reason to assume that He would expect any less of us?

If you have a plan or a vision of what your dream will look like once it comes to pass, I encourage you to write it down. If you haven't done this yet, you have been missing out on a golden opportunity. Committing your ideas to paper is the easiest way to begin assessing what it will take to see them accomplished. It is also the best way to keep track of all of those small moments of inspiration that can be so easily lost to the passing of time. Your don't need to wait until you have all of the details perfect to start. Begin where you are, write down what you know, and allow God to inspire you to greater depths of vision and understanding.

Then the Lord answered me and said: "Write the vision and make it plain on tablets, that he may run who reads it (Habakkuk 2:2).

Writing down your vision is important for many reasons. It will keep you accountable to yourself as you continue to make progress in your preparations. It will give you a clear vision of the planning and work that still needs to be done. It will also help you to remember and keep track of each important detail as your plans progress. But perhaps the most important function of a written plan is its ability to inform and inspire others. As we are about to see, that is exactly what David's plan did for the rulers and leaders who heard it:

Then the leaders of the fathers' houses, leaders of the tribes of Israel, the captains of thousands and of hundreds, with the officers over the king's work, offered willingly. They gave for the work of the house of God five thousand talents and ten thousand darics of gold, ten thousand talents of silver, eighteen thousand talents of bronze, and one hundred thousand talents of iron. And whoever had precious stones gave them to the treasury of the house of the Lord (1 Chronicles 29:6-8a).

Upon hearing David's words – upon seeing the details of his preparation, and the extent of his passion for this beautiful dream – all of his subjects, the leaders of the various houses of Israel, were inspired to contribute to the cause as well. They willingly offered unthinkable amounts of gold, silver, jewels, and bronze for the building of the temple of the Lord.

Isn't it incredible to consider the effect that David's dream had on these men? It started off as a personal passion, an intimate desire to do something to honor God. But when he began to share it with the people around him, they took the dream on as their own. Men of power and influence looked at the great work that David was preparing for, and it awoke within them a desire to join the mission. His dream was no longer just his own. He had inspired others to partner with him in taking action.

This is a theme that you will see running through the lives of many of the Bible's dreamers, and I believe that it is one of the most beautiful aspects of the dreams that God gives His children. We already know that our dreams are meant to impact many lives. Isn't it wonderful to realize that the impact that they might have is to cause others to begin dreaming as well?

David had a dream in his heart, but it was not something that he could accomplish on his own. In fact, God was the one who stopped him from attempting to complete it in his own power. He was left, instead, to prepare and to plan for a task that he would eventually pass along to his son. But the beautiful thing was that he was able to present his dream to the people, not as something that he had done by himself, but as something that he was entrusting to them to complete without him. By handing off his dream to those would come after him, David gave them the opportunity to take part in something bigger than themselves. He gave them a dream that they could achieve!

It is important to realize that just like David, your role in fulfilling the dream in your heart may not always look exactly the way that you'd first envisioned. In fact, as your dreams grow and expand under God's hand, you may find yourself in a position where it becomes impossible to do it all alone. But that doesn't mean that your dream is dead, or that you should give up on it. On the contrary, if God has put the dream in your heart, then it is because you are essential to its success. Finding the way to contribute to that dream sometimes means making a way for others to play the parts you'd planned for yourself. Do it anyway, and trust that God will give you a level of joy and satisfaction that will fill you to overflowing. Never forget that when you do things God's way, they will always turn out better than you ever could have imagined.

But no matter what you do, take hold of your dream now as if it were coming to you tomorrow. Live your life in preparation for the promise that is to come. Take ownership of the passion that the Lord has planted in your heart, and steward it well. Don't let it go cold. Don't let the routine of everyday life distract you from your purpose. Work, study, prepare, and plan with all your might, just like David did. Teach yourself, train yourself now to excel. The work that you do today will pave the way into your future.

ACT

NEHEMIAH'S BOLDNESS

❖❖

One of the central themes that has run through the stories of our dreamers up until this point it has been the idea of delay. Each of the men and women we've learned about so far experienced a period of waiting before they were able to realize their dreams. Each of them endured a time during which their dream was put on hold.

But it is important for us to recognize that while waiting may sometimes be a necessary part of our journey, and while we should make sure that we maintain the right perspective when we face those times, the truth is that the path to our dreams has never been about the waiting. In fact, if you go back and read the stories of Hannah, Moses, Caleb, and even David you will notice that the Bible spends virtually no time discussing these waiting periods. Years, even decades of delay are virtually ignored in the Biblical account of these dreamers' journeys. Why do you think that is?

The simple answer is that the waiting didn't matter. What was important to God was not the time that these people spent on hold. What mattered was the actions that they took when those periods of delay ended. When the restraints were lifted off of their lives, they all took steps to actively pursue their goals. Each of these dreamers made the choice to take bold, specific action that propelled them into their dreams. It was their decisions to do something, to move forward, to take risks, and to walk in faith that made them successful and led them to their destinies.

This is one of the most fundamental differences between an ordinary dreamer and a dream chaser. Everyone has a dream. But dream chasers are people who actively run after their dreams, no matter what. That simple willingness to act is often the only thing that stands between our success and failure.

Don't forget that it was an immobility provoked by fear that ultimately kept the Israelites out of Canaan for forty years. It wasn't the obstacles they faced. It wasn't even that God didn't want them to go. On the contrary, He was actively trying to push them forward into their victory. Nevertheless, the Israelites exiled themselves from their own dreams by a simple choice not to act. Their success was lost the moment that they refused to move forward.

Without the willingness to take action, we will never take the steps necessary to claim the dreams that God has placed in our hearts. Remember that He is the One who gave us the impossibly grand, incredible, and beautiful dreams that we treasure. He didn't give them to us to torture or tease us. His plan is to fulfill each one of those dreams, but He needs our cooperation in order to see it done.

Following God takes courage. It is not a path for the faint of heart. There will be times when He presents us with opportunities that can launch us into our destinies, but grabbing hold of those destinies may involve risks that we don't feel properly prepared to take. It might mean stepping out of our comfort zones, away from the familiar, and into uncharted territories. The question that we must ask ourselves is this: am I ready to take bold action in pursuit of my dream, even in the face of risky and uncertain circumstances?

My hope is that you are already prepared to say yes and to take full advantage of every chance that God provides for you to move into your promises. Of course we must make sure that our actions are never sinful, deceitful, or in conflict with God's word. We know that we are responsible to walk in the light and to act with integrity. But that does not disqualify us from taking bold, decisive action when an opportunity presents itself. On the contrary, knowing that we are doing our best to walk in the will of God should empower us and make us bolder. After all, if we are in His will, we have the confidence of knowing that He will support, direct, and (if necessary) adjust us along the way.

Don't be afraid to take courageous steps towards the dreams that God has given you. Don't be afraid to reach further, to take risks, or to act boldly. Doing so can launch you into places that you might not have dreamt possible. It will lead you along paths that you would never have imagined, much less planned to take. In short, the willingness to boldly and aggressively pursue your dream is essential if you are serious about reaching success.

One of my favorite examples of this basic truth is found in the story of Nehemiah. His life provides an incredible testimony of what can happen when a man or woman of God takes bold initiative in the pursuit of the dreams in his or her heart. From his life we can learn how to speak, operate, and move forward with courageous faith – putting our trust entirely in our Almighty God, and taking full advantage of every opportunity that He provides for us to move forward towards our dreams.

Nehemiah lived in the time when the nation of Judah had been removed from their land and brought into captivity in Babylon. The majority of his people were, like him, prisoners and captives living in this foreign land. The place that they had once called home, the land of Judah and it's capital city of Jerusalem, were far behind them. The temple where they once worshiped God was nothing but a memory. His once mighty nation had been utterly ruined, and the strength of his people was gone.

Then one day, travelers came to visit Jeremiah from what was left of the land of Judah, bearing even more bad news:

And they said to me, "The survivors who are left from the captivity in the province are there in great distress and reproach. The wall of Jerusalem is also broken down, and its gates are burned with fire."

So it was, when I heard these words, that I sat down and wept, and mourned for many days; I was fasting and praying before the God of heaven (Nehemiah 1:3-4).

When Nehemiah heard about the state of Jerusalem, the capital city of his once powerful nation, it broke his heart. He was suddenly confronted with the reality of what was happening in his homeland. His people were destitute. His nation was destroyed. The servants of the Great I Am were seen as failures, and the Lord's once-beautiful temple was demolished.

The idea that the city of Jerusalem and the temple of God were lying in ruins was horrifying to Nehemiah. He could not abide the thought that anyone would look at the people of God and see them in reproach.

In that moment a dream was birthed in his heart. It wasn't a rational dream. It wasn't something that he had any reason to believe that he would be capable of achieving. In fact, it was so far removed from his reality that it might as well have been impossible. Nevertheless, in that moment, Nehemiah's despair was countered by a desperate hope: a hope that he might somehow bring his people back to the land of their forefathers and restore the city of Jerusalem to its former glory.

Now we have to understand that Nehemiah was not a powerful or influential man. He was a captive, a servant in a strange land. He had no riches, no prestige, no resources with which to accomplish this dream. He worked as a servant in the king's household, but he was not an advisor or a governor. He knew that the king was the only one who could help him, but he had no reason to expect that the king would ever take notice of him, much less give him an audience. So he did the only thing that was in his power to do: he turned to God in prayer and asked for His help. He understood that his dream was so impossibly large that the only way it would happen would be if God moved on his behalf.

Not long after Nehemiah began to seek the Lord about finding a way to fulfill his dream, he was given an unexpected opportunity. Nehemiah worked in the palace, where he served as cupbearer to the king. And it wasn't long before the king took notice of Nehemiah's change of countenance, and asked him why he seemed so sad.

Now I had never been sad in his presence before. Therefore the king said to me, "Why is your face sad, since you are not sick? This is nothing but sorrow of heart."

So I became dreadfully afraid, and said to the king, "May the king live forever! Why should my face not be sad, when the city, the place of my fathers' tombs, lies waste, and its gates are burned with fire?" (Nehemiah 2:1b-3)

That moment proved to be a launching point in Nehemiah's life, but we must recognize that from his perspective it was a terribly frightening and dangerous one. The kings of of this land were not common or ordinary men. They were held in such high regard that even entering the throne room without permission was grounds for immediate execution *(Esther 4:11)*. For the king to notice Nehemiah, a mere servant, was a dangerous thing. For him to comment on Nehemiah's sad countenance was enough to set him into an understandable panic!

It's hard for us, as members of a modern and free society, to understand the dangers that Nehemiah faced in that moment of confrontation. He was not free to speak his mind without the very real risk of serious consequences. If what he said angered, displeased, or even annoyed the king, his life could be taken from him in an instant.

It took an incredible act of boldness for Nehemiah to tell the king the truth in that moment. By admitting that his sorrow came from the state of his conquered city, he risked implying that he was also displeased with the king, rebellious against his authority, and even dissatisfied with the honor of his position in the palace.

Nevertheless, Nehemiah put aside his fear, placed his life on the line, opened his mouth and spoke the truth. The burden of his dream was so heavy on his heart that it could not be hidden. It was all over his face! So rather than lying, rather than pretending that everything was fine, Nehemiah took bold action. He told the king what was in his heart.

Then the king said to me, "What do you request?"

So I prayed to the God of heaven. And I said to the king, "If it pleases the king, and if your servant has found favor in your sight, I ask that you send me to Judah, to the city of my fathers' tombs, that I may rebuild it"
(Nehemiah 2:4-5)

I would imagine that when Nehemiah opened his mouth and admitted that he was mourning the destruction of his city, the last thing he would have expected was for the king to ask him what he wanted to do about it. But that's exactly what happened! Suddenly, a situation that had just been terribly frightening took a remarkable turn. Instead of the death sentence he'd feared, Nehemiah was suddenly presented with an profoundly powerful opportunity. The king of Babylon, the one person with the means to make Nehemiah's dream come true, was literally asking him to name his request.

In that moment, Nehemiah had very little time to think. He didn't have the chance to consider his options or talk it over with his friends. He had no time to plan, to formulate a careful response, or to weigh a list of pros and cons. It was a now-or-never moment, one that he knew would never come again. And so Nehemiah took yet another bold step – he said a quick prayer, and then asked the king to let him go home to rebuild Jerusalem.

The Bible doesn't tell us what Nehemiah prayed in that moment, but it doesn't take a scholar to make an educated guess. It certainly wasn't a long prayer. It probably wasn't even said out loud. My best guess it that it went something like "Lord, please don't let me screw this up!" or "Please give me the words to say so I don't get myself killed!" Whatever it was that Nehemiah asked for in that moment, it was enough. It gave him the strength, the courage, and the faith to tell the king what he wanted. Even though he was completely unprepared for this moment, even though it had probably never even occurred to him that he would ever get such a chance, Nehemiah refused to miss his opportunity. He was willing to risk his very life for the chance to see his dream come to pass.

This story has an incredibly practical application for our pursuit our own dreams. While we may never be put in a life or death situation while chasing our dreams, we must recognize that God sometimes opens doors in sudden and unexpected manners. When He does, there will not always be time for us to sit back and wait until we are comfortable with our circumstances. In fact, we may face moments when we don't even have time to do more than say a quick prayer before we leap into the unknown. But if we can be bold enough if our faith to lay hold of those opportunities and claim those moments, they can bring us to places that even a hundred years of careful planning would never produce.

It is not a bad thing to be taken by surprise by the opportunities that God will give you. It's even ok to be unsure whether you're saying or doing the exact right thing when those opportunities come. I would imagine that Nehemiah was terrified throughout this whole encounter with the king. But the one thing that you don't want is to allow that trepidation and surprise to paralyze you. Prepare yourself now. Make the decision that you will be a risk-taker, and that you will not let those moments go by without seizing every opportunity to move forward into the destiny that God is offering you!

Then the king said to me (the queen also sitting beside him), "How long will your journey be? And when will you return?" So it pleased the king to send me; and I set him a time (Nehemiah 2:6).

Here's the thing about the risk that Nehemiah took – it totally paid off! Despite the fear, despite the uncertainties, despite all of the things that could have gone terribly wrong, Nehemiah got exactly what he wanted. The king granted his petition, right then and there. In fact, the Bible says that it *pleased* the king to send him on this crazy quest to Jerusalem!

This brings us to an important point, one that I'd like to take the time to explain more fully. We know the Bible is a natural telling of factual events. But more than that, it is a message from God regarding our spiritual lives. So when we read this story we recognize that while this king before whom Nehemiah served was a real man who existed in history, he is also a representation of our King, the One before whom we serve – Jesus Christ.

So when this scripture tells us that the king was pleased to grant Nehemiah's request and send him on the path towards his dream, it is doing more than showing us how God moved upon the heart of a natural king to grant Nehemiah favor and make a way for his dream to come true. This scripture is actually a demonstration of the very real pleasure and joy that God in heaven, your King, finds in granting the absurd and impossibly large requests that you, His servant, make of Him.

Even when we know better, there are still times when we as Christians may feel like the things we want are too big, too wonderful, or even too personal for God to bother granting to us. We deceive ourselves into believing that He is too busy, too far-removed, or too focused on other, more "important" things to bother with our requests, our dreams, or our needs. But nothing could be farther from the truth. The king in this story (who represents Jesus Christ) took notice of Nehemiah's sadness. He saw his sorrow of heart and took the time to address it personally. What's more, when he granted Nehemiah's request it actually gave him pleasure to do it. It gave him joy and satisfaction to answer his petition!

What an incredible picture this paints of God's attitude towards us. It shows us that our personal fulfillment is important to Him – important enough for Him to come to us and ask us what's wrong, even when we're too afraid to approach Him first. He doesn't wait for us. He pursues us. He wants us to speak to Him about our dreams, about our fears, about our sorrows and about our hopes. He wants us to take these things to Him because it pleases Him to answer us. He enjoys giving us our blessings and our breakthroughs!

So never allow yourself to believe that you are beneath God's notice. No matter how trivial your issues or your dreams may seem in your own estimation, God wants to hear about them. He wants you to tell Him what's bothering you. He wants you to cast your cares on Him. That is how you open the door for Him to bless you in that area; and it is His good pleasure to grant you those blessings, even when you think you don't deserve them.

But let's go back now to Nehemiah and his encounter with the king:

Furthermore I said to the king, "If it pleases the king, let letters be given to me for the governors of the region beyond the River, that they must permit me to pass through till I come to Judah, and a letter to Asaph the keeper of the king's forest, that he must give me timber to make beams for the gates of the citadel which pertains to the temple, for the city wall, and for the house that I will occupy." And the king granted them to me according to the good hand of my God upon me (Nehemiah 2:7-8).

I'll say this much for Nehemiah – he had guts. The king had already spared his life, listened to his absurd request, and granted him permission to leave the palace and return to his homeland to rebuild his capital city. Most of us would have considered that a win, and run out of the room before the king changed his mind; but not Nehemiah. He recognized that this was his once-in-a-lifetime opportunity, and he was determined to get everything out of it that he could possibly manage. Once he had opened his mouth, and once he saw that he was being granted unfathomable favor, he refused to leave until he had asked for everything he could possibly need for his journey, everything that he could think of that would help him to complete his goal.

Nehemiah wasn't satisfied with permission to go and rebuild Jerusalem. He also asked the king to give him the resources that he would need to complete the task. He requested permission to use wood from the king's own forests to do the work. Could you imagine asking the ruler of your land for permission to rebuild a city that had been conquered and torn down, and then, after he said yes, requesting that he give you the money to do it? As if that wasn't enough, he even asked for additional resources so that he could build himself a place to live while he was there!

But as incredible as it seems, God gave Nehemiah favor with this king, and every single request that he made, no matter how outrageous it sounded, was granted to him. Can you imagine if he hadn't been so bold in making his requests? Could you imagine if he'd been content to leave for Jerusalem without those resources? How much easier did his task become simply because he exercised the courage to ask for what he needed?

Nehemiah was a very bold and daring man. He was not fearless – in fact, the Bible specifically tells us that he was very much afraid when this encounter started. But he did not allow his fear to paralyze him into inaction. He did not let it stop him from pursuing the opportunities that God put before him. In fact, he pursued them with such zeal, such boldness, and such fervor that he left the king's presence with everything that he could possibly need to see his dream become a reality. His boldness awarded him not only an open door, but the power, authority, and resources to get things done.

Nehemiah walked into work that morning a sad man with an impossible dream. He walked out, though, with a completely new identity. The entire landscape of his life transformed in a matter of minutes, all because he boldly and aggressively pursued the possibility of his dream. In fact, it was not just his own landscape, his own future that was changed. When he arrived in Jerusalem, he came with the power and the influence to transform the futures of every Israelite that he found living there.

Then I said to them, "You see the distress that we are in, how Jerusalem lies waste, and its gates are burned with fire. Come and let us build the wall of Jerusalem, that we may no longer be a reproach." And I told them of the hand of my God which had been good upon me, and also of the king's words that he had spoken to me.

So they said, "Let us rise up and build." Then they set their hands to this good work (Nehemiah 2:17-18).

Imagine for a moment what it must have felt like to be an Israelite living in Jerusalem at this time. Only the poorest and least important people had been left behind – everyone with any skill, education, or influence had been carted off to Babylon long ago. Those who remained were leaderless, hopeless, and oppressed – doing their best to eke out a living amid the squalor and the rubble of a city that they were not allowed to even attempt to rebuild.

But when Nehemiah arrived, their hopeless lives were suddenly given new meaning. When they looked at him they did not see the broken man who'd wept for his city with little hope of ever saving it. They did not see the frightened servant who'd trembled as he told his dream to the king. What they saw was one of their countrymen returning to Jerusalem with an entourage of men, the favor of the king, riches and resources beyond their comprehension, and a plan to rebuild their ruined city, and with it their lives!

No wonder these people agreed to work with him. His arrival must have been a very real answer to their prayers; and I am sure that there was more than one man among them who had also been quietly dreaming of the day that Jerusalem could be rebuilt. Nehemiah's boldness, his courage in the face of fear had an impact that went beyond his own life. It put him in the position to be an example and a leader among his people. It gave him the ability to empower and inspire them, to pull them out of the squalor in which they had been living, and to encourage them to work and dream for something better.

However, this is not the end of Nehemiah's story. He did not ride into Jerusalem a hero and then rest easy. His work was far from over. In fact, he was forced to fight every day just to keep his dream alive.

You see, there were leaders and governors living in the land who did not want Nehemiah to succeed. They were so determined to see him fail that they went to extreme lengths to sabotage the work that he and the Israelite people were doing. They tried attacking the city. They tried appealing to the king. They tried threats and intimidation. They even tried to ruin Nehemiah's character! Things got so bad that the men building the wall wore armor and carried swords while they worked and while they slept. They had to be prepared to defend themselves at all times in case an attack came.

But Nehemiah had the Lord on his side, and he was determined to see his dream fulfilled. He chose to live every day with the courage and the boldness to move forward towards his dream, no matter what opposition he faced. This facet of Nehemiah's courage is incredible, and again offers us an important lesson. You see, he had been bold when he stood before the king, and again when he returned to Jerusalem. But this was the first time that Nehemiah faced any real opposition while pursuing his dream. It was the first time that anyone actually tried to stop him.

But this very real and very dangerous threat had no effect on Nehemiah's courage. He was bold enough in his conviction to continue working, no matter what threats were made against him. He was so focused, so single-minded in his purpose that aside from enacting safety precautions to protect his workers, he never gave his enemies a second thought. In fact, when they tried to trick him into meeting them so that they could harm him, his answer was perfect in its simplicity and honesty:

that Sanballat and Geshem sent to me, saying, "Come, let us meet together among the villages in the plain of Ono." But they thought to do me harm. So I sent messengers to them, saying, "I am doing a great work, so that I cannot come down. Why should the work cease while I leave it and go down to you?" (Nehemiah 6:2-3)

I love everything about Nehemiah's response to these men. He was too focused on the great dream that he had been building to waste time paying attention to the petty plans of the enemies who were trying to stop him, so he quite literally refused to lower himself from the height of his purpose to meet them at their level.

Nehemiah would not be baited. He refused to be distracted. He would not allow these petty, carnal men take his eyes off of what was important. They tried to lie to him, to start rumors about him, to trick him into doing something sinful. His response was simply to ignore them!

That perspective saved Nehemiah from a lot of trouble. It kept him from getting himself tangled in traps and schemes that could have made his life very difficult. But he understood a truth that ran deeper than the plots of these men. He knew that God was on his side, and that gave him the courage and the boldness to chase after his dreams in spite of the obstacles that these wicked men were attempting to throw in his way.

Ignoring our critics can be such a difficult thing. Our natural reaction is to want to fight to defend ourselves. But when people mock us, criticize the work that we are doing, or try to bait us into useless arguments or fearful defenses, the best thing that we can do is refuse to come down. God does not need us to defend Him, and in truth we do not need us to defend ourselves – the Lord has us covered on that front.

So when the attacks come, when the jeering and the skepticism come, when the rumors start and people try to use them to manipulate you, remember what Nehemiah said. Don't see opposition as a sign of failure, see the attacks as a sign that you are doing something right. Follow his example, and refuse to come down. Have the courage to keep your mind and your eyes on the higher things to which God has called you, and let the baser matters work themselves out on their own.

So the wall was finished on the twenty-fifth day of Elul, in fifty-two days. And it happened, when all our enemies heard of it, and all the nations around us saw these things, that they were very disheartened in their own eyes; for they perceived that this work was done by our God (Nehemiah 6:15-16).

By the end of Nehemiah's story, he had fully achieved the dream that was in his heart. Jerusalem's wall was rebuilt. The city was restored. The Israelite people were successful. Their enemies were disheartened. And even the surrounding nations understood that what they had witnessed was a move of God.

Even though Nehemiah had no reason at the beginning of his dream to think that it would ever be possible, God made a way through that impossibility that led him directly into success. The only thing that was required of him was the courage to keep moving forward. He did not let fear stop him. He did not let opposition or oppression stop him. He didn't let anything hold him back. Instead, he boldly walked through every open door, and courageously moved forward every single day until the dream was his.

What a wonderful example this man has set for us to follow! If you have a dream in your heart, no matter how big or how small it may seem, give it to God. Then, when God opens the door in front of you, have the courage and conviction to walk through. When He lays a path before you, have the character to walk down it, and continue to follow it every day until your reach your dream.

We must always remember that our dreams are never too far out of reach for us to achieve them. We simply need to be prepared, as Nehemiah was prepared, to take bold action when God provides us with the opportunity. If we are willing to follow after God, to walk through the open doors that He provides for us, then He will be faithful to see us through to the end, to the fulfillment of our most impossible dreams.

So no matter what your path looks like, don't be distracted by obstacles or attacks. Don't allow fear to paralyze you into inaction. Move forward with God. Follow where He leads. Refuse to stop, no matter what. Boldly claim what He is giving you, and in the end you will find yourself in a place of victory!

TRUST

JOSEPH'S UNWAVERING FAITH

❖

It would be unfair to write a book about chasing our dreams without taking the time out to discuss what happens when things go wrong. It's easy to imagine that following a God-given dream will mean instant success and quick payoffs for you hard work. Sometimes people's dreams do come that way. But those are not the only stories that exist in the tapestry of dreams and dreamers.

In fact, if you look at the stories of the dreamers whom we have studied so far you will notice a pattern. Before their dreams became a reality, each one faced disappointments, obstacles, hardships, or trials. Hannah suffered torment at the hands of her rival for years before she received her breakthrough. Caleb, through no fault of his own, was shut out of his dream for an entire generation. Even Nehemiah started his journey while he was living as a captive in a foreign land.

These people faced tough times and discouraging circumstances, problems that might have caused lesser men and women to despair of ever seeing their dreams fulfilled. Their stories ended in victory, but none of them began that way. First, God had to reach into each of their lives and turn their greatest tragedies into testimonies. He breathed life back into the very areas that seemed most dead. Despite the apparent hopelessness of their situations, He gave them each the very dreams that had once seemed impossibly out of reach.

This is such an important pattern for us to recognize before we begin to chase our dreams. Without it, every problem, every obstacle can seem insurmountable. But once we realize that even apparent tragedy or catastrophe cannot deny us our dreams, we will be able to face even the most difficult times with the right perspective. We will be able to endure even the hardest of trials, and we will not be moved.

The truth is that things won't always go the way you want them to go. In fact, there may be times when things will go so terribly wrong for so long that you won't be able to imagine how God could ever get you out of the mess you're in and back onto the path to your dreams. That doesn't mean that you've failed, or that God has forgotten you. It doesn't mean that your dreams are over, or that you are beyond His reach. It simply means that your story isn't finished yet. You still have something great to look forward to.

The most important thing that we can do when we face these difficult times is to keep our eyes on Jesus. Focusing on Him – on His word, His promises, His faithfulness, and His goodness – is essential if we are to endure the rockier pathways along the journey towards our dreams. If we get caught up in our surroundings, if our eyes are fixed on our circumstances, we can lose track of the greater truths that God has given us. But when we keep our eyes on Jesus, when our relationship with Him overshadows our natural realities, we will not only survive the trials and setbacks that we face, we will thrive.

Perhaps the greatest example in the Bible of this level of faith and relationship with God is found in the life of a man named Joseph. Most of us already know Joseph's story. He was, after all, the ultimate dreamer. As one of Jacob's twelve sons, he had inherited the promise that God had first given to his great grandfather, Abraham – that he would become a great nation and a blessing to the world. As his father's favorite, he was used to receiving incredible favor and special treatment. So when Joseph had a dream that he would rule over his brothers, it probably seemed like the most natural thing in the world to him:

So he said to them, "Please hear this dream which I have dreamed: There we were, binding sheaves in the field. Then behold, my sheaf arose and also stood upright; and indeed your sheaves stood all around and bowed down to my sheaf" (Genesis 37:6-7).

The dream in Joseph's heart came to him in the form of a literal dream. As he slept God gave him a vision of his brothers' sheaves of grain bowing down to his. As far as dreams go, this one was relatively easy to interpret. Joseph woke up believing that one day he was going to rule over his brothers, and he embraced this vision of his future with joy.

Of course Joseph's brothers, who already hated him for the preferential treatment he received from their father, were outraged to hear about this dream. To them it sounded like the empty boasts of an arrogant child. There was no reason for them to believe in the future Joseph saw for himself. He had no grounds to stake such a claim. In their eyes, his words and his dream were nothing but trouble.

Perhaps Joseph was unwise to share it with them in the manner that he did. But that does not change the fact that this dream, however contentious or impolitic it may have seemed, was from the Lord. Isn't it interesting to consider that God gave this man a dream that the people around him found offensive? Looking at the situation from a natural perspective, these men saw Joseph's desire as aggressive, arrogant, and inappropriate. But it clearly came from God! How could a God-given dream be any of those things?

The answer, of course, is that it couldn't. The dreams that He gives His children are always good. They are always for the benefit of many. They are designed to be a blessing!

This is something that we should keep in mind when we are dealing with other Christians and the dreams that God has given them. We may not always understand their dreams. They may, at times, seem to be inappropriate, aggressive, self-centered, or impossible. However, no matter how they appear to our natural eyes we should always be careful not to mock, deride, reject, or scorn them. We don't want to react the way that Joseph's brothers reacted. We do not want to dismiss or interfere with God's plan simply because we don't understand it.

Then he dreamed still another dream and told it to his brothers, and said, "Look, I have dreamed another dream. And this time, the sun, the moon, and the eleven stars bowed down to me."

So he told it to his father and his brothers; and his father rebuked him and said to him, "What is this dream that you have dreamed? Shall your mother and I and your brothers indeed come to bow down to the earth before you?" (Genesis 37:9-10)

If there was any doubt in Joseph's mind that this dream was from the Lord, it was settled when God gave him a second dream with the same meaning. Once again he saw representations of his family bowing down and honoring him, and once again he shared this dream with them.

Now we all know what happened next, but before we get to that part of the story, I'd like to take the time to consider Joseph's dreams from his perspective. Have you ever wondered what he thought they would mean, or how he imagined them coming to pass? Of course he had no idea what his future would look like. Still, if he was anything like us, Joseph had probably spent some time daydreaming and imagining the path that he would take in order to see his dream become a reality.

What must that path have looked like in his mind? I'm just speculating, of course, but I can imagine that he pictured a traditional rise to power within his own family structure. He probably thought that he would be given more and more responsibility and authority within the household, until he was eventually named his father's heir and his family's new head. Perhaps he imagined that his brothers would slowly come to respect him and accept his leadership, or that he would do something wonderful to win their love and admiration. I'm sure that however he imagined getting there, it was, in his mind, the ultimate culmination of a series of successes and victories. He had no way of knowing that his dream would come to pass only after he had faced a lifetime of wrongs, failures, and disappointments!

It didn't take long for things in his life to start going badly either. Not long after he told his family about his dreams, his brothers decided to get revenge. Fueled by hatred and jealousy, they found him alone in the field one day and sold him as a slave to some passing Midianites:

Then Midianite traders passed by; so the brothers pulled Joseph up and lifted him out of the pit, and sold him to the Ishmaelites for twenty shekels of silver. And they took Joseph to Egypt (Genesis 37:28).

Joseph's brothers, the men who shared his blood and his home, hated him so much that they tied him up and sold him like a piece of property to a group of strangers who were passing by. Talk about the ultimate form of betrayal! Talk about a terrible turn of events. Whatever ideas Joseph may have had about reaching his dreams, I'm sure that they never included anything like this!

Suddenly Joseph found himself in a horrible situation, one that he never could have anticipated. The life-path that he'd imagined following on the way to his dream had taken a sharp turn, and was suddenly headed directly towards disaster. No rational person could possibly have seen this as anything short of a tragedy, and I'm sure that Joseph must have seen it that way himself. In one terrible day he had been stripped of his family, his home, his inheritance, his security, his freedom, and even his humanity. He had ceased to be Joseph, son of Israel. He had instead become a slave, a possession to be bought and sold.

Eventually Joseph was brought to Egypt where he was sold to a man named Potiphar. It was there, in a foreign land, where Joseph began his new life. I'm sure that in those first few days he had a million questions and just as many fears. Everything that had once seemed stable was now in chaos. Everything that had ever mattered to him was gone. In the midst of the confusion and fear, I would imagine that Joseph struggled with a specific and poignant question: where was God?

The Bible doesn't leave us in doubt about this though. It actually answers the question directly:

The Lord was with Joseph, and he was a successful man; and he was in the house of his master the Egyptian. And his master saw that the Lord was with him and that the Lord made all he did to prosper in his hand. So Joseph found favor in his sight, and served him. Then he made him overseer of his house, and all that he had he put under his authority (Genesis 29:2-4).

Where was God? He was right there with Joseph! Isn't that incredible? Even when Joseph was facing the darkest and most hopeless days of his life, the Bible tells us that the Lord there was with him. He was not alone. God's hand was upon his life, still guiding and sheltering him. As a result he began to find success, even though he was a slave. In fact, he was so successful that even his master was able to recognize God's hand upon him.

But that didn't happen all at once. When he first arrived in Egypt, Joseph didn't have any visible sign of God's presence in his life. In fact, anyone looking at his circumstances might easily have assumed that God had rejected him. After all, he was going through the worst experience imaginable – and all as a result of an unthinkable betrayal. How could someone going through something so terrible still be within God's will and experiencing His favor?

This is a point that requires some consideration on our part, because it can be so easy to use the circumstances in our lives as measuring-rods for God's favor over us. When things are going well we assume that God is well pleased with us and working on our behalf. As soon as things start to go badly, however, we begin to question. We wonder what we did wrong to deserve the problems that we are facing. We ask God why He would let such terrible things happen to us, why He is punishing us, or why He won't just swoop down and rescue us.

However, Joseph's story demonstrates to us very clearly that it is possible to experience God's favor and His blessings even when everything in our lives is going wrong! In other words, our circumstances, no matter how wonderful or how terrible, are not a barometer of our relationship with the Lord. Bad situations are not necessarily a sign of separation from God. They are not always evidence that we have wandered off course. We cannot, therefore, allow our circumstances to move us – not when it comes to our faith in God. If we are grounded first in our relationships with Him, the trials and problems that we face will lose their power to shake us from our foundation.

As time progressed and Joseph found more favor in his master's eyes, he was eventually given the responsibility to oversee Potiphar's entire household. God's favor elevated him and set him apart, even within the confines of his slavery. But this brought with it a new problem. As Joseph rose to prominence, he caught the eye of Potiphar's wife, and she decided to seduce him. This woman was aggressive and insistent. She knew what she wanted, and she was not ready to take no for an answer. It eventually reached a point of confrontation where Joseph was forced to address the matter directly:

But he refused and said to his master's wife, "Look, my master does not know what is with me in the house, and he has committed all that he has to my hand. There is no one greater in this house than I, nor has he kept back anything

from me but you, because you are his wife. How then can I do this great wickedness, and sin against God?"
(Genesis 39:8-9).

I love Joseph's objection to this woman's advances. I love that he had the character to do what was right, even when a person of authority was pressuring him to do what was wrong. I love that he was horrified at the thought of betraying the man who had been kind and generous to him, who had entrusted him with so much. But more than anything, I love that even as a slave in a foreign land he still steadfastly refused to sin against God.

In this simple statement we see one of the great keys to Joseph's success. He did not use his circumstances as an excuse to turn away from God. Despite the very real struggles that he faced, he was still as committed as ever to living a righteous and holy life. Even though his dreams seemed impossibly out of reach, he was still faithful to the One who had given them to him. No wonder Joseph experienced such favor! No wonder God's hand was so clearly present in his life. He was faithful to the Lord, even when things were not going well. What a wonderful example for us to follow!

Of course we know that we do not serve God simply because of the blessings that He gives us. So when we face times of struggle, when our lives seem to be in shambles, and our dreams are impossibly far away – in those times of testing, we must cling to Jesus even more. We must make the quality decision to honor Him even in the midst of our own disappointment and shame. When we are able to do that, we will see His hand moving. His favor and His grace will guide us through the most difficult of situations.

Joseph's life, however, was about to take what would look like another wrong turn. In yet another act of terrible and unjust betrayal, his master's wife did not take the rejection well. She lied to her husband about Joseph – claiming that he had attacked her. As a result, his master grew angry and threw him into prison *(Genesis 39:20)*.

Even though Joseph had still done nothing wrong, he was once more faced with another life-altering setback. Every success that he had won was once again stripped away from him. His sterling reputation was smeared with the most terrible of lies. And as if that weren't bad enough, he found himself a permanent prisoner in an Egyptian jail.

But the Lord was with Joseph and showed him mercy, and He gave him favor in the sight of the keeper of the prison. And the keeper of the prison committed to Joseph's hand all the prisoners who were in the prison; whatever they did there, it was his doing (Genesis 39:21-22).

Once again, Joseph found himself in a terrible, unjust, and degrading circumstance; but once again the Bible explicitly tells us that the Lord was right there with him! Things had only gotten worse, but God was still very present. What that meant, of course, was that as bad as the situation seemed, it was exactly where Joseph was supposed to be. In that moment, in that terrible situation, Joseph was perfectly positioned to move forward towards his dream. Even though everything looked wrong, the truth was that it couldn't be more right!

This brings us to another point, a simple truth with incredible significance: we cannot fix what isn't broken. It is easy to see our negative situations as problems that need to be fixed, or as the consequences of some terrible mistake. But that is not always the case. There are times when the most negative situations in our lives may be the very ones that God plans to use to launch us into our dreams.

Now of course I would never discount the fact that we do face consequences for our actions, and many of the sticky spots we find ourselves in are directly linked to the mistakes we've made to get ourselves there. Moses' life taught us that lesson. But sometimes you will find that the situation you're in is not of your making, and that there is nothing to fix that will get you out. Don't let that discourage you. Know that sometimes the valleys you encounter are less about what you've done to get there and more about the mountaintops you will find on the other side. Sometimes God leads us into difficult seasons and situations not because they are a consequence of our past, but rather because they are a conduit to our future.

Joseph, spent years in slavery and was now facing imprisonment in a foreign land for no reason other than the higher purposes and plans of God. From an objective viewpoint, having heard the full story, we understand that those many long and terrible years were God's way of getting him to the right place at the appointed time. He was brought through the valley so that he could be lifted up to untold heights on the other side.

But imagine what it must have felt like for Joseph, sitting in a filthy prison cell, wondering how he'd gotten himself into such a terrible spot. Imagine if Joseph had spent that time struggling to find out what he needed to fix in order to get himself out of the mess he was in, or searching for the lesson that God was trying to teach him. He would have found nothing but frustration and failure – because as terrible as the situation was, it did not need fixing. God had him there for a purpose and for a set time in order to accomplish great and miraculous things through him. In fact, even as Joseph found himself in the worst situation he'd experienced yet, God was already setting into motion the very events that would bring him out of tragedy and into the dream that he had been promised so many years earlier.

After Joseph spent some time working in the prison, he was given custody of two new prisoners. One had been the Pharaoh's chief butler, and the other his chief baker. One night these two men both had dreams that confused and frightened them. When he heard about their dreams, Joseph offered to help them, trusting in God to give him the interpretation:

So Joseph said to them, "Do not interpretations belong to God? Tell them to me, please" (Genesis 40:8b).

Once again Joseph took advantage of an opportunity to glorify the Lord, and in doing so he demonstrated his absolute assurance in God's goodness and faithfulness. He never questioned whether the Lord would interpret their dreams. He had complete faith that the One he served would show up on behalf of these men.

But where did Joseph get this confidence in God? It could not have come from his experiences. After all, his experiences up until this point had been terrible. The confidence, rather, was an outgrowth of his faith. He knew that God would not abandon these men because he knew that God had not abandoned him. He had faith that the Lord would answer their prayers because he exercised that same faith for his own life every single day.

Joseph never lost his faith. Even after everything he'd endured he still believed that God would redeem him. It didn't matter that years had gone by, or that things looked worse than ever. Joseph knew that his story wasn't over yet, and that his trials would not last forever. He believed in the future that God had promised him more than he believed in the circumstances in which he found himself. He understood that the power of his problem was nothing in comparison to the power of his God. He held on to his dreams, the ones that God Himself had given him so long ago, and he refused to let them go.

With this confidence, Joseph heard from the Lord and interpreted the dreams of both the butler and the baker. After he had finished interpreting the butler's dream, assuring him that he would be returned to his position in the Pharaoh's house, he asked him for one small favor in return. Just like Nehemiah, Joseph was bold when he was given the opportunity. He asked the butler to remember him once he had been released, and to go to Pharaoh on his behalf:

But remember me when it is well with you, and please show kindness to me; make mention of me to Pharaoh, and get me out of this house ... Yet the chief butler did not remember Joseph, but forgot him (Genesis 40:14, 23).

I don't know about you, but I find it appalling that this man could forget Joseph so quickly and so easily. After all, Joseph had reached out to help the butler when he was alone and afraid, befriending him when he had nothing, and giving him hope in an otherwise hopeless situation. But even after he begged the butler to remember and help him, the man completely forgot about Joseph as soon as he was set free. The man was restored to his status in the palace, while Joseph remained in the prison. Yet another person in Joseph's life had let him down.

In fact, it wasn't until two years later, when Pharaoh had a dream that couldn't be interpreted that Joseph even crossed the butler's mind (*Genesis 41:1*). This time, however, Joseph's life was finally about to change for the better.

The Bible tells us that the butler told Pharaoh about Joseph, and about how he had correctly interpreted his dream, and that Pharaoh immediately sent for him and had him brought to the palace.

Imagine what that day must have been like for Joseph. I'm sure that he woke up that morning just as he had day after day, year after year, expecting nothing more than to continue his work in the prison. He was dirty. He was unkempt. He was probably wearing rags. He very likely smelled terrible. Then suddenly guards appeared at the prison door asking for him by name. He was whisked off to the palace, where he was bathed, shaved, given real clothes to wear, and then ushered into the throne room of the most powerful man alive, who began to ask him about his ability to interpret dreams. Talk about a whirlwind experience!

So Joseph answered Pharaoh, saying, "It is not in me; God will give Pharaoh an answer of peace" (Genesis 41:16).

In the midst of this crazy and unbelievable turn of events, Joseph did what he always did – he gave glory and honor to God. He made sure that Pharaoh knew that it was not by his personal might or wisdom that he was able to do anything, but only because of the goodness of the God whom he served.

Joseph went on to give the Pharaoh the interpretation of his dreams. He explained to him that God had sent the dreams as a warning, and that after seven years of bounty, the land of Egypt and the surrounding region would suffer through seven years of terrible famine. He then went on to advise the Pharaoh that it might be wise to begin collecting food immediately to store up for the years when it would become so scarce.

Then Pharaoh said to Joseph, "Inasmuch as God has shown you all this, there is no one as discerning and wise as you. You shall be over my house, and all my people shall be ruled according to your word; only in regard to the throne will I be greater than you." And Pharaoh said to

Joseph, "See, I have set you over all the land of Egypt" (Genesis 41:39-41).

The Pharaoh's reaction to Joseph's interpretation and advice is the stuff of fairy tales. He was so amazed at Joseph's insight and wisdom that he immediately put him in charge of the entire nation of Egypt. He recognized, just like Potiphar and the prison keeper had before him, that Joseph was someone special. His circumstances, his status didn't define him, even in the eyes of these completely carnal people. So even though Joseph was a prisoner, a slave, and a foreigner, he was instantly promoted past all of the king's officials and made second in command of the entire nation.

When God changed Joseph's situation He did it in sudden and extraordinary fashion. Joseph woke up that morning a slave and a prisoner; but he went to sleep that night as the ruler over all the land of Egypt. Joseph had waited for years without seeing anything that even resembled progress towards his dream. But when the moment was right, when God opened the door, his life was completely transformed in a matter of hours.

The realization of Joseph's dream, when it finally came, was grander and more far-reaching than his initial understanding of it had ever been. He had dreamed of ruling within his family, but God had destined him to rule over multitudes! Just like so many other dreamers in the Bible, Joseph started off with a vision of something small, and God transformed it into something world-changing. His dream became a blessing not just to him, but to entire nations of people who might otherwise have starved.

Eventually the Pharaoh's dreams came true. Just as Joseph had predicted, after seven years of prosperity, the land fell into a devastating famine. There was no food to be found anywhere, and people from Egypt and all of the surrounding lands came to Joseph to buy the food that he had been storing in anticipation of their need.

Joseph's brothers eventually came as well, and although they did not recognize him, they did make his dream a reality by bowing down before him *(Genesis 42:6)*. The story of their reunion is long and complex, but eventually Joseph had all twelve of his brothers in front of him, and he revealed himself to them.

His brothers were understandably afraid. After all, the last time they had seen him they threatened to kill him, threw him into a pit, and eventually sold him into slavery. Suddenly they discovered that the boy they'd once betrayed had become the most powerful man in Egypt – a person who could have them all executed with just a word!

However, Joseph was quick to put his brothers at ease:

"But now, do not therefore be grieved or angry with yourselves because you sold me here; for God sent me before you to preserve life ... So now it was not you who sent me here, but God; and He has made me a father to Pharaoh, and lord of all his house, and a ruler throughout all the land of Egypt" (Genesis 45:5, 8).

Joseph reassured his brothers with an incredible statement. He told them that it was not their treason that had sent him to Egypt, but God's plan. He explained to them that what had happened was necessary, that he had needed to go through all of those dark and difficult years. He understood that those terrible times were an integral part of the path that led him to the fulfillment of his dream, and he saw that it was God's hand that had brought him through.

Joseph's path to his dream was a long and painful one. He was brought as low as a person could possibly go before God was able to bring him to the pinnacle of power, authority, and prestige. But what is most remarkable about Joseph's tale is the incredible attitude that he maintained throughout the darker years of his life.

Even though he was wrongfully treated and abused at every turn, we never read that Joseph spoke even one word of complaint, doubt, or fear. No matter how terrible his situations became, Joseph always found a way to work hard, to make the best of it, and (most importantly) to give honor and glory to God. No matter how far out of reach his dreams appeared to be, he never let go of the One who had given them to him in the first place. He did not let his problems define him. Instead he pressed on, always trusting that God was going to make a way for him.

No wonder God was able to entrust him with the power to rule over all of Egypt! This man had such incredible character, such unwavering faith, that it's hard to imagine living up to his example. But his story is told in the Bible for our benefit. It is a beautiful demonstration of the importance of keeping our eyes on Jesus.

Don't be afraid of failure or setbacks. They happen. They may happen more than once. That does not mean that God has abandoned you, or that you cannot achieve what

He has placed in your heart. If the door doesn't open the way you expect, if you get set down, remain faithful in your heart, in your words, and in your deeds to the Lord, and to the vision that He's given you.

Know that the way is being made for a greater testimony in your life. Never doubt it. Never allow anything to tear you away from that truth. The God whom you serve is faithful and just. He will make a way for you, even when there seems to be no way. All you need to do is keep your eyes focused on Jesus. Cling to your faith, trust in your Lord, and He will bring you through the valley and onto the mountaintop on the other side.

EXPECT

Abraham's Anticipation

❖

There is one last dreamer in the Bible whose story I would like to share with you before we end. In his tale there is a final lesson that we can learn about living our lives as dreamers and as dream chasers. In this man's story you will recognize many of the themes that we have already touched on throughout this book. You will see reflections of Hannah's need to expand her vision and Moses' failed attempts to achieve his dream by the wrong means. You will recognize Caleb's undying zeal and Joseph's constant faith. But what strikes me most about this story is the incredible expectation with which this man lived. Although he wasn't perfect, he reached the point where he genuinely believed that God was going to show up and do the impossible on his behalf; and from that moment forward he lived in active anticipation of his miracle. This is the story of Abraham and his dream of having a son.

Nor shall your name any longer be Abram [high, exalted father]; but your name shall be Abraham [father of a multitude], for I have made you the father of many nations (Genesis 17:5 AMP)

Abraham, as you may know, did not start off as Abraham, but as Abram. Abram, which literally meant *high, exalted father*, was the name he carried with him since his birth. It was an especially powerful and meaningful name. Unfortunately it was also an ironic one, because it represented the one thing in his life that Abram was unable to attain on his own. He and his wife could not have children, and his one desire was to have a son to whom he could pass down all of the incredible blessings that the Lord had bestowed upon him.

But when God renamed Abram and called him Abraham, a name which meant *father of a multitude*, it was symbolic of a greater promise, an expanded dream that He was offering to him. You see, God wasn't satisfied with making Abram into a father. He wanted Abram to become Abraham – literally a father of nations. One son was Abram's dream, it was all he ever wanted. However, God wanted to give him descendants that would fill and bless the earth.

In fact, this incredible expanded dream had actually been given to Abram many years before his name was changed:

But Abram said, "Lord God, what will You give me, seeing I go childless, and the heir of my house is Eliezer of Damascus?" Then Abram said, "Look, You have given me no offspring; indeed one born in my house is my heir!"

And behold, the word of the Lord came to him, saying, "This one shall not be your heir, but one who will come from your own body shall be your heir." Then He brought him outside and said, "Look now toward heaven, and count the stars if you are able to number them." And He said to him, "So shall your descendants be" (Genesis 15:2-5).

Years before Abram became Abraham, God had already started to shift and expand his vision. Abram met with God and asked Him why He was bothering to bless him, since he had no children to inherit his fortune. He was placing his unfulfilled dream at God's feet and asking for an answer. God reacted, as He does so often, by expanding and multiplying Abram's dream. Instead of promising him the one son he wanted, God offered Abram descendants as numerous as the stars in the sky. In that moment, seeing the vast expanse of the heavens stretching to the horizon and filled with more stars than he could count in a lifetime, Abram embraced God's greater plan. He allowed his vision to be expanded, his dream to be reshaped.

From that point forward, Abram understood that he didn't have to convince God to give him his dream. On the contrary, he saw that this dream, the one that was so close to his heart, had been given to him by God as a part of His larger purposes. Just like Hannah, Abram embraced the fact that the fulfillment of his dream was going to affect more than just his own life. God was planning on using him to bring forth a nation through which the entire world would be blessed!

But as is often the case with the promises we see God fulfilling in the Bible, Abram's dream did not come to pass right away. Years went by, Abram got older, and still he had no son. The descendants that God had promised him where nowhere to be found. So after enduring a literal lifetime of barrenness, Abram and his wife, Sarai, got tired of waiting. They decided they would find their own way to produce an heir, and in the process, they compromised the integrity of their dream.

Now Sarai, Abram's wife, had borne him no children. And she had an Egyptian maidservant whose name was Hagar. So Sarai said to Abram, "See now, the Lord has restrained me from bearing children. Please, go in to my maid; perhaps I shall obtain children by her." And Abram heeded the voice of Sarai ... So Hagar bore Abram a son; and Abram named his son, whom Hagar bore, Ishmael (Genesis 16:1-2, 15).

There is an incredible point in this verse that is often overlooked, but it is one that is worth mentioning. We know that God had explicitly offered Abram a son. But at the same time, according to Sarai, He had also closed her womb. He had literally restrained her from having the very child that He'd said she would bear. This strange paradox put Abram and Sarai into a difficult situation, one in which they had to decide just how much they were willing to entrust into God's hands.

It is not at all uncommon for God to offer us promises that are so vast, so unfathomably great, that they seem absolutely unachievable. And it is no less common for Him to then restrain the very methods by which we would expect to see those promises fulfilled in our lives. When we find ourselves in that frustrating, seemingly hopeless situation, our job is simple. All we need to do is wait on God and follow His direction. He does not need us to manufacture a solution to the problem. We don't have to figure out a natural way around the restraints. All we need to do is trust and obey, remembering that the Almighty One who has promised us the impossible is more than able to remove every barrier to the fulfillment of that promise.

Unfortunately, Sarai's reaction when faced with this situation was all wrong. Rather than waiting on God, she grasped for a carnal solution to the problem in order to manufacture her husband's blessing. She came up with the idea of giving Hagar, her servant, to Abram so that he could bear a child by her. That is, of course, the polite way of saying that Sarai encouraged her husband to sleep with one of the servants and get her pregnant.

If you think that sounds like soap opera material, you're right! Even by today's standards, Sarai's proposal was shockingly inappropriate, and the fact that a man as righteous as Abram agreed to it seems unfathomable. It's hard to imagine the many rounds of rationalization and justification that Abram and Sarai must have gone through in their minds to eventually bring themselves to the point of agreeing on such a misguided action.

After all of those years of waiting, it is easy to guess that they were feeling more than a little frustrated. They knew that God wanted them to have a son. They hadn't forgotten His promise. However, after trying time and time again, they hadn't made any headway. As they got older, it must have felt like their time was running out. Eventually they developed such a desperate need to see something happen that they took the dream out of God's hands and took action on their own.

But as we learned from Moses, attempting to achieve God-given dreams by carnal methods will never work out well. While Abram and Sarai's plan did end up producing the expected results – Abram did have a son – it was far from the solution that they'd been hoping for. Hagar's pregnancy upset the balance in their lives and caused all sorts of strife within their home. It caused Hagar to act pridefully, Sarai to act vindictively, and Abram to act foolishly. This one misguided decision completely ruined the happiness and peace of the entire household. Their carnal solution to Sari's barrenness ended up creating more problems than it solved.

So Hagar bore Abram a son; and Abram named his son, whom Hagar bore, Ishmael. Abram was eighty-six years old when Hagar bore Ishmael to Abram.

When Abram was ninety-nine years old, the Lord appeared to Abram and said to him, "I am Almighty God; walk before Me and be blameless. And I will make My covenant between Me and you, and will multiply you exceedingly." (Genesis 16:15-17:2).

Perhaps the biggest problem that Ishmael's birth created is also the one that is easiest to miss – specifically the sudden silence that Abram experienced from God. Abram was eighty six years old when he had Ishmael, and as soon as he had his son, things went quiet. In fact, the Bible skips ahead thirteen years in a single verse, immediately jumping to the next time that God spoke to him.

But that period of waiting cannot be so easily dismissed. I, for one, cannot help but wonder what it was like for Abram during that time. On the one hand, of course, it may not have seemed much different than the waiting he had been doing before Ishmael was born. After all, he was seventy five years old when he first began to follow after God, and even before then he must have desired a son and known that it was beyond his reach.

On the other hand, however, I cannot help but think that this particular time of waiting must have been especially difficult, because before this he'd had no reason to imagine that God would deny him the son that He had promised. Of course, we know the end of this story, so we know that God did not have any intention of withholding Abram's blessing. But sometimes I wonder, did Abram know it? Or is it possible that he believed that his dream, his promise, was dead and gone?

I'd like to encourage you to put yourself in Abram's shoes for a moment and consider what may have been going through his head as those thirteen years went by:

He knew that he'd sinned – that he had made a terrible mistake. He knew that Ishmael was not the son that he had been promised, and that God disapproved of the manner in which he was conceived. In one foolish and weak moment, Abram had taken the matter into his own hands and attempted to create his own solution. The results were a disaster. And to make matters worse, God had suddenly stopped speaking to him.

Do you think maybe Abram managed to convince himself that'd he'd disqualified himself from his dream? Do you think as the days, months, and years of silence continued to pass that he gave up on ever hearing from God again? Do you think he ever believed that he'd messed up too badly to ever find his way back into God's favor?

If Abram was in any way like the rest of us, I can't help but imagine that this was an especially difficult season for him – filled with doubts, fears, guilt, and regrets. He may very well have abandoned any hope of ever having the son that God had promised. He may have done what the Shulamite woman did, and buried his dream, trying to forget it ever existed.

However, this season did not last forever. Thank the Lord that He is not willing to abandon us to our mistakes. His dreams and desires for us remain unchanged, and even when we have done everything imaginable to mess things up, He is still willing to move on our behalf.

After thirteen years of silence, God returned to speak to Abram. But amazingly, it wasn't to chastise or punish him. His encounter with Abram did not include a single word of rebuke or condemnation.

God was not interested in punishing Abram. He did not speak to him of his past sins or mistakes. Instead He simply said, *"walk before Me and be blameless."* In other words, God was telling Abram that it was not too late. If he would walk in obedience from that point forward, God was still ready to honor His covenant and give Abram his dream.

I am amazed every time I consider the implications of this example for our lives as Christians today, and I truly believe that the point it makes cannot be overstated. The point, of course, is that it is not too late for you to achieve your dream.

You may have made mistakes, and those mistakes may have done incredible damage to your life or severely limited your future. You may have even done things that you knew were in direct disobedience to God. But you must understand that your sin, however terrible, cannot chase God away or change His mind. He is not interested in punishing you; if He were, there would have been no need for the cross. Instead, He is always actively looking for the chance to make your life right again, to reestablish His covenant with you, and to bring you into the future that He has created for you. He is still speaking to you, just as He spoke to Abram, and offering you the opportunity to walk before Him and be blameless.

This moment of reconciliation was the point when God chose to change Abram's name to Abraham. That simple act forever solidified Abraham's identity as a father of nations. Even though he and his wife were still childless, even though they were older than ever, and even though they had hopelessly mangled their promise by interfering with God's greater plan, He had arrived to tell them that their dream was still very much alive. Abraham and Sarah could still expect see descendants as abundant as the stars, just as God had promised them so many years before. Abraham's past had not destroyed his future. In fact, he was on the brink of receiving everything that he had ever wanted.

Then Abraham fell on his face and laughed, and said in his heart, "Shall a child be born to a man who is one hundred years old? And shall Sarah, who is ninety years old, bear a child?" (Genesis 17:17)

Abraham's reaction to God's announcement was understandable. If I were him, I would probably have laughed too. The suddenness of it all must have seemed so absurd, so unbelievable, that I'm sure Abraham wondered if he'd heard right. After ninety nine years of barrenness, after thirteen years of silence, after he had buried that dream away deep in his heart, suddenly God appeared and said, "It's time! I'm about to give you your dream."

But again, this very relevant story reflects back onto our own lives when we consider the promises of God in light of what we believe to be possible. It forces us to reexamine our expectations, to go back and look at the promises that God had spoken into our lives already.

I'd like to challenge you to take a moment right now to go back to the dreams that God has already given you, and to ask yourself a few questions. What is the most laughable thing that God has ever promised you? How laughably large is the extent of your dream? What absurd and unreachable blessing did the Lord say that He would give to you? And what was your reaction when you heard it? Did you scoff? Did you sneer a little bit? Did you question? It's ok if you did – so did Abraham, so (later on) did Sarah, and so have I on more than one occasion. The limited capacity of our human thought makes such a reaction almost impossible to avoid. Even the father of faith had his moment of skepticism. But he was wise in that he refused to allow that laughter to turn into doubt.

It is time for us to reevaluate our concept of the impossible. There are so many things that God has promised us, so many dreams that He has birthed in our hearts that may be beyond our ability to comprehend. The very act of accepting His word in those moments may often require us to stretch our faith. And yet somehow we know beyond a shadow of a doubt that those promises came from God. What is it, then, that makes us want to put limits on the reach of His hand? What, exactly, is it that we think Him incapable of?

There is nothing impossible for the Lord. So do not toss the promises of God aside or treat them lightly. When they are so large, so great, so far-reaching that you could never imagine their fulfillment, rejoice! And when God interrupts your life in order to revisit the promises and dreams that you thought were long-dead, be glad! His timing is perfect, and His reach is infinite. If He is stirring and awakening the dreams within your heart it is because He intends to fulfill them.

And Abraham said to God, "Oh, that Ishmael might live before You!" (Genesis 17:18)

In that moment, Abraham was so shocked at God's pronouncement, that he did the strangest thing; he actually tried to convince God to bless Ishmael and to transfer the promise to him, the son born of compromise. From an objective standpoint it is, of course, easy for us to see the foolishness of such a request, but it demonstrates very clearly the difficulty that Abraham had in believing that he and Sarah would ever have children of their own. Even as he stood before the Lord and received a confirmation of the promise he had been given so long ago, Abraham still expected that he would have to to settle for a compromise. He still thought that God would only be able to bless him through Ishmael.

"No, Sarah your wife shall bear you a son, and you shall call his name Isaac; I will establish My covenant with him for an everlasting covenant, and with his descendants after him. And as for Ishmael, I have heard you. Behold, I have blessed him, and will make him fruitful, and will multiply him exceedingly. He shall beget twelve princes, and I will make him a great nation. But My covenant I will establish with Isaac, whom Sarah shall bear to you at this set time next year" (Genesis 17:19b-21).

What I love about this particular scripture is that God heard Abraham's plea, and His grace was so perfect that He was willing to extend His blessing even over the life of Abraham's illegitimate child, the son of compromise. The Lord did indeed make Ishmael a great nation. In fact, He gave him a lineage that included twelve powerful princes, and a country that thrived for hundreds of years.

But even though He was willing to bless Ishmael, God insisted that His covenantal promise would manifest through Isaac, the son who still had not come. In that simple declaration, God not only confirmed His covenant with Abraham, but once again plainly told him that it was through the son of promise, the son that he had been dreaming of for so long, that his true lineage would be established.

In other words, God absolutely refused to allow Abraham to settle for anything less than the complete fulfillment of his dream. Thank God that He was not willing to compromise the way that Abraham was! Despite Abraham's doubt, the Lord was not about to lessen the fullness of His promise. He was not about to withdraw the blessing that He had offered all those years before.

I believe that many of us may find ourselves in Abraham's position at some point in our lives. We have dreams in our heart that once seemed so ripe with promise. But time passed us by, and those dreams never came any closer. Maybe we made mistakes along the way that left us with messy consequences. After the passage of so much time, after all of the things that we've done wrong, we eventually come to the point where we have trouble believing that God will actually make a way for us to see our dream come to pass. It becomes almost too good to believe. So when the moment comes, when God says, "now is the time," we laugh, we scoff a little bit, and we attempt to find a compromise that seems *good enough* given the failings of our past.

However, even when we feel completely unworthy, even when our dreams feel more out of reach than ever, and even when we can't really believe it, God is still invested in seeing those dreams become reality. He is not interested in leaving us with second best. God will never give up on your dream. Don't allow yourself to give up on it either.

After this encounter with the Lord, everything changed in Abraham's life. Up until this point he had been Abram, the high exalted father of no one. But from this moment forward he became Abraham, the father of nations. With this change of name came a new perspective, a new level of faith, and a new understanding of the reality of God's promises.

Abram was a man who had been willing to believe in the vision of God's plans for his life; but only up to a point. When time and fear got the best of him, he made a mistake. He lost his confidence in God's plan, and ventured out to fulfill one of his own making.

Abraham, on the other hand, had a complete understanding of the power of God's word, and absolute faith that His promise would come to pass. He had gotten over the fear and the doubt, and he was ready to move forward into a future that included of the birth of his long-dreamed-of son. Nothing was going to stand in his way. Nothing was going to distract him from his purpose. Abraham had ceased thinking of himself as the victim of his mistakes and circumstances, and began living as a victor, confident that his God was going to make a way for his dreams to become a reality.

Then the Lord appeared to him by the terebinth trees of Mamre, as he was sitting in the tent door in the heat of the day. So he lifted his eyes and looked, and behold, three men were standing by him; and when he saw them, he ran from the tent door to meet them, and bowed himself to the ground (Genesis 18:1-2).

When God finally came to Abraham to give him the realization of the dream that he'd held for so long, He found him sitting by the door of his tent in the heat of the day. To me that just speaks such volumes about Abraham's new level of expectation. You see, the heat of the day was a time for rest. It was a time that people spent napping or relaxing in the coolest, shadiest parts of their tents. Certainly, no one would be expecting visitors at that hour. So why was Abraham sitting by the door, staring into the sun? Why wasn't he resting with his family? Well, the Bible doesn't actually tell us this, but I like to believe that he was sitting there in expectation of his visitation from God.

You see, Abraham had dream from God that needed to be fulfilled. And even though it had been years, and even though he had tried and failed to work out his own solution, it seems clear that this time around Abraham was not willing to forget or give up on his promise. He understood that God was going to give him his breakthrough. It was only a matter of time.

In fact, he was so sure that God would stay true to His word, that he was actually sitting at his door, waiting for

Him to arrive! No wonder this man is known as the father of faith! His dream was beyond impossible. In fact, it grew more impossible every day; but he refused to let it fade into his past. He spent his time actively looking for his miracle. He never stopped expecting God to move on his behalf.

Can you imagine that? Can you imagine Abraham waiting at the door of his tent every day expecting that *this* would be the day that his dream came true, that *this* would be the day that God would show up for him? What an incredible example of faith that would be – never to be downtrodden, never to be defeated, but waking up every morning with fresh faith and new hope saying, "I'm one day closer to receiving my promise!"

I don't know about you, but if I have to spend any time waiting for a dream from God, I'd rather spend it in joyful anticipation than depression and disappointment! I'd rather wake up every morning believing and celebrating the fact that God is moving on my behalf, and knowing that my dream is closer today than it was yesterday. That kind of faith does not take some extraordinary force of will or inhuman spiritual strength. It comes when we learn to simply take God at His word.

That's what Abraham did. He finally came to the place where he believed that God would do exactly what He said He would do. He believed it so completely that he spent his time actively looking for God to show up on the scene. He sat at the door of his tent, waiting for God to come change his situation.

As a result, when God actually arrived, He found Abraham already at attention, already expecting his answer. And just as God had promised, it was not long before Abraham and Sarah bore a child:

For Sarah conceived and bore Abraham a son in his old age, at the set time of which God had spoken to him. And Abraham called the name of his son who was born to him—whom Sarah bore to him—Isaac (Genesis 21:1-2).

Abraham's walk with God wasn't perfect. He made terrible mistakes. For a while he even despaired of ever seeing his dream come to pass. But in the end, he received his son of promise. He saw his dream come true. But this only came after he had undergone a change in identity. He had to leave the old man, Abram, behind, and step into the identity that he had been given by God. He had to become Abraham, the father of multitudes. He had to see himself from that viewpoint and believe that God would make it a reality. He had to live and walk in faith, believing that his dream was on its way.

Only after that transformation took place was God able to open Sarah's womb and give them the son that they had so desperately wanted. Abraham's dream became a reality when he allowed God to transform him from a dreamer into a dream-chaser. It happened when he began to live his life in expectation of his dream.

So let's follow Abraham's example. Let's pursue our dreams, not just with passion and zeal, but with confidence and unshakable faith. Let's take God at His word. Let's believe that He is the good father He claims to be, and that

He desires to bless us. Take hold of your promises, cling to your dream, and be like Abraham – waiting with baited breath for God to show up for you. Embrace the expectation within your heart, and renew the fire that once burned inside you. But whatever you do – don't give up because you are one day closer to receiving your promise. Your dream is on its way!

CHASE

Your Challenge

❖

Throughout the course of this book we have learned about the lives of men and women who dared to live in pursuit of the dreams that God had placed in their hearts. These people were not perfect. Just like us, they made mistakes, faced frustrations, and sometimes even got themselves stuck along the road to their dreams. But each of them found a way to persevere until they achieved the purposes to which God had called them. Because of this, they each stand as an example of what can be achieved when we align ourselves with the Lord's greater purposes and follow after His plans.

However, this book is more than an exploration of what has happened in the past. It is meant to challenge you to move forward towards your future. We didn't spend time reading about these people's lives simply because we like or admire them. We did it because we want to emulate them. We've attempted to learn from their examples because we want to achieve similar successes in our own lives. We too desire to see our dreams become reality. With that in mind, I would like you to look back at each of the people that we have met along this journey, and allow the lessons that they taught to provoke you to action.

HANNAH

The first person we learned about was Hannah. Her story taught us the importance of giving God ownership of our dreams so that He can expand them. Her example showed us how even the most personal dream can be transformed into something powerful enough to bless a nation. If she had not been willing to offer her dream up to God, if she had not committed her unborn son to His service, Samuel would never have been born, and Israel would have missed out on one of the greatest prophets to ever live.

Hannah's story teaches us that it is not enough to dream for our own sakes. If God has given the dream to us, then we must be willing to surrender it back to Him so that it can be used for a greater purpose. When we do that, it will enable Him not only to bring our dreams to pass, but also to expand and multiply the blessing, both in our lives and in the lives of countless other men and women. Allowing God to expand your dream – giving up your control over it – is one of the first and most daring steps you can take in your journey towards its completion.

You may have dreams in your heart that are so personal that you can't imagine them having an impact on anyone other than yourself. That's ok. Hannah had a dream just like that – all she wanted was a child. But she was willing to give her dream over to the Lord for His purposes anyway. Are you willing to do the same thing? It can take time to learn how to let go, especially of dreams that we have held so close to our hearts for so long. But you can start by prayerfully asking yourself these questions, and allowing God to show you the answers:

- What is my heart's first desire, to please and honor God, or to receive blessings that He can give me?
- Who can my dream bless, besides myself?
- Have I asked God what changes He might want to make to my dream?
- Do I earnestly believe that God's plans for my life will lead me to fulfillment and joy?
- Is there something that God has asked me to give Him that I don't want to give up? Can I ask Him to help me to trust Him with it?
- Have I looked for ways to use my dream to be a blessing to others?
- Am I willing to surrender my dream back to God, to give it up if He asks me to?

MOSES

From Moses we learned that the only way to achieve the dreams that God has given us is by doing things His way. Moses saw his people suffering in slavery, and he desired to set them free. But he made a mistake when he first attempted to liberate them. He tried to do it by methods that were not godly – he attacked and killed one of their oppressors. He thought that the Israelites would recognize him as a deliverer. He probably imagined that they would rally around him in revolt against their Egyptian masters, but that was not God's way, and it led to disastrous consequences.

As a result of his rash and carnal actions, Moses had to leave Egypt and hide in the desert for forty years. God eventually redeemed him and restored his dream to him. He did become the deliverer he desired to be. But Moses had to wait for decades before his dream became a reality. In the end, it only happened when he submitted himself to God's direction and followed His plan, rather than doing things his own way.

If our dreams are a part of God's greater plan, then we can be assured that He has devised a way to see them come to pass. As soon as we attempt to fulfill God-given dreams by the world's methods, however, we run the risk of creating natural obstacles and hindrances that God never intended us to face. We can put our dreams on hold, delaying the very things that we are trying to achieve, simply by going about things the wrong way.

Remember that if God has given you a dream, then He will provide a righteous, honest, and Biblically sound means of achieving that dream. Following the path that He has for you is the only sure way of reaching your goal. Are you pursuing your dream with integrity? These questions will help you focus on doing things God's way, rather than your own:

- Have I done anything to compromise the integrity of the dream that God has given me?
- Are the choices I'm making in pursuit of my dream aligned with the character of Christ? Are they the choices that Jesus would make?
- Are there things that I would do differently if I knew that others would see and know about them?
- Do I ever try to hide or deny my sins or mistakes?
- Am I willing to do things God's way, even if it means waiting?
- Do I seek God's guidance when making plans, or am I focused on figuring them out for myself?
- How do I treat other people while I'm pursuing my dream? Does my treatment of them reflect the love of God?
- Is there an area in my life where I have allowed sin to hold me back from God's will?
- Do I trust that God's plan will ultimately lead me to success? Or do I think I need an alternate plan, just in case?

CALEB

From Caleb we learned that we must live the life of a victor, that we must be passionate and confident in our own success as we chase after our dreams.

Caleb was one of the spies who were originally sent into Canaan to survey the land for the Israelites. When he came back, he and Joshua were ready to go in at that very moment and claim the promised inheritance that God had given them. They knew that they could defeat any enemy, because God was on their side. But because the rest of the Israelites were afraid and refused to go, Caleb had to wait over forty years before he was allowed to enter into the promised land and claim his inheritance.

Nevertheless, even after all of that waiting, Caleb was as ready when his moment arrived as he had been when he'd first returned from his survey of the land. It didn't matter that he was over eighty years old, or that he'd watched an entire generation of men die in the wilderness. He had the same mentality of victory that he'd had as a young man. He was just as passionate and aggressive about pursuing his dream as he had been when he first insisted that God would make the people victorious. And by God's grace he was able to overcome his enemy and take possession of the very mountain that God had promised him forty years earlier.

It's important for us to remember that we are not chasing our dreams by purely natural means. If we have given our dreams to God and are pursuing them according to His direction, we have every confidence that He can and will make a way for us. We do not have to measure our skill against our task, or our strength against that of our enemies, because God is on our side, and there is nothing that can stand in our way or hold us back when He is forging our path.

Are you zealous about pursuing the dreams that God has placed in front of you? Do you have the same confidence as Caleb? Here are some questions to help you evaluate and (if necessary) rediscover your passion for your dreams:

- What factors, barriers, or circumstances in my life discourage me from pursuing my dream?
- Are those factors bigger or more powerful than the God I serve?
- Do I listen to negative voices? How do I respond when people speak negatively about my dream, or my chances of achieving it?
- Do I ever allow myself to meditate on doubt-filled or fearful thoughts?
- If my dream came tomorrow, would I be ready to claim it?
- Have I allowed my passion or zeal for my dream to fade? How can I keep that zeal alive and thriving?
- Have I held back from doing the things that God has prompted me to do in pursuit of my dreams?
- What has God asked me to do that I've avoided starting because I was intimidated or afraid?

DAVID

From David we learned the essential lesson of living each day in active preparation for the dreams that we have not yet realized. David was restrained from building a temple for the Lord. God Himself told David that he would not be the one to see his dream through to its completion. His son, Solomon would be the one to build the temple instead.

However David didn't let that stop him from working towards that dream for the rest of his life.

He spent every day preparing, planning, and gathering resources, so that when the time came for his son to construct the temple, everything would be ready for him. He didn't let even the smallest detail escape his notice, and he made sure to write down a meticulous plan for Solomon to follow. Is it any wonder, then, that his men were inspired by his passion and joined his cause? Of course not! It's certainly no surprise that Solomon eventually created a temple that was so majestic that it became famous all over the world. David's dream became a reality, and even though he wasn't there to see it completed, his preparation is what made it possible.

Most of us will never find ourselves in David's shoes, where God Himself holds us back from our dreams. We may, however, find ourselves in the more common position of being unable to actively pursue our dreams for a season. That is not a bad thing. In fact, it is a opportunity that we should embrace. If you have not yet achieved your dream, take advantage of the time that you have been given every day. Use it to begin to plan and prepare yourself, so that when your dream does come, you will be ready. Don't put this off until tomorrow or next year. Begin now!

Remember that the seeds of preparation that you plant today will produce a harvest of success in your future, and it is often those who take the time to prepare and plan in advance who find themselves best equipped to thrive when their dreams become reality. Now is the time to start preparing for your dreams. Here are a few questions to help you get started:

- What work or planning can I begin to do now in preparation for my dream?
- What will I need (information, education, resources, money, relationships, etc.) when my dream arrives?
- Is there anything about my character or personality that God wants me to adjust while I'm waiting for my dream?
- How many of those things can I begin to work towards now? What simple actions can I take right away to begin my preparations?
- What have I done today to prepare for my dream?
- Have I written my dream down? Have I created a written plan of action?
- If my dream were to come tomorrow, would I be ready? How can I ensure that I will be more ready tomorrow than I am today?

NEHEMIAH

From Nehemiah we learned how important it is to be willing take bold steps in the pursuit of our God-given dreams. Nehemiah dreamed of rebuilding the walls of Jerusalem despite the fact that he was a virtual nobody, a servant in a foreign land. He had no reason to believe that his dream was possible. However, when he was given the sudden chance to present his petition to the king, he took full advantage of the opportunity. He not only asked for permission to go back to Jerusalem and rebuild the city, but when he saw that he had favor in the king's eyes, he continued making requests – reaching for more and more until he received all of the resources and authority that he would need to finish the job.

Once he arrived back in his homeland, Nehemiah continued to boldly pursue his dream, despite the fact that he was surrounded by men who were determined to stop him. In fact, he was so focused on his task that he refused to stop his work long enough to engage in their pettiness or acknowledge their threats. His confidence in the Lord was so strong that he did not worry about his own self defense, his reputation, or his safety. In fact, he refused to take his eyes off of the work until he saw his dream completed and his city restored.

There is so much that we can learn from Nehemiah's bold and aggressive pursuit of the dream that God had given him. There are times when we will need to be willing to take courageous steps in order to see our dreams come true. We cannot allow fear or timidity to hold us back in those moments. We must step out in faith when our opportunities present themselves. Don't ever be afraid to boldly ask for what you need, to speak to those who have the power to open doors in your life, or to press every advantage that God gives you in your pursuit of your dreams.

Once those opportunities arrive and we find ourselves moving forward our courage must continue. We may face opposition or even attacks from those who don't want to see us succeed. That does not mean that we should stop. In fact, if we are following Nehemiah's example, we will continue to press forward, working fearlessly towards our goals until we see them accomplished.

Know that if God is for you, no one can stand against you. Decide now that you will be bold and courageous as you chase after the dreams that God has planted in your heart. You can begin to evaluate and adjust your perspective with these simple questions:

- Am I prepared for the fact that God may suddenly present me with an opportunity to advance my dream?
- Am I willing to take bold action in pursuit of my dream, even if it involves risk?
- When God shows me the next step to take in pursuit of my dream, will I do it? What if it is something that pushes me outside of my comfort zone?
- How would I react if opportunity came tomorrow? Would I respond in fear or in faith?
- Am I ready to speak up and ask for what I need, even when I don't deserve it and have no reason to expect it?
- Do I believe that I have the favor of God over my life?
- Do I allow other people's opposition to distract or dissuade me from pursuing my dream with all of my heart?

JOSEPH

From Joseph we learned how essential it is to keep our eyes focused on Jesus and to trust Him no matter what our circumstances look like. Joseph started off with the dream of one day ruling over his brothers. Little did he know that the path that would lead him there would include threats to his life, slavery, false accusations, imprisonment, and a string of betrayals! At the time these events must have seemed to be the most terrible tragedies, but they were the only possible path that Joseph could have taken to reach his ultimate position as ruler over all of Egypt.

The most amazing thing about Joseph's journey, however, was the attitude that he maintained throughout it all. No matter what he faced, no matter where he found himself, he always worked diligently, lived with integrity, and above all, trusted in and honored God. He may have struggled with sorrow and discouragement. He may have wondered how he had ended up in such terrible positions. But he steadfastly refused to let his circumstances destroy his faith. In fact, the Bible gives us every indication that his relationship with God was the one thing that remained constant throughout the peaks and valleys of his life.

Like Joseph, you might not always find yourself in ideal circumstances while you are pursuing or waiting on your dreams. In fact, it is entirely possible that things in your life may go terribly wrong somewhere along the way and leave you in a place where your dreams no longer seem possible. But don't let that discourage you. The problems of your past and the issues of your present cannot define or determine your future. No matter what your life looks like today or tomorrow, there is still a dream waiting on your horizon, and God has every intention of seeing it fulfilled.

You serve a God who is all-powerful, all-knowing, and actively working on your behalf. He knows the dreams that you have. After all, He is the one who gave them to you. So keep your eyes on Him no matter what. Let your relationship with Him be the foundation that you lean on. It is the only thing in your life that is guaranteed not to crumble. If you trust in Him, He will bring you through the trials and the battles. Not only that, but He will give you the very dreams that may have once seemed unobtainable.

Have you been living in faith like Joseph? Challenge yourself to go deeper, by asking yourself these simple questions:

- Have I let my circumstances take my eyes off of God and His unfailing love for me?
- When problems happen, is my first instinct to run to God or away from Him?
- Do I ever see the negative situations in my life as a sign that I have done something wrong, or that God is punishing me?
- Have I ever used the problems in my life as an excuse to ignore or walk away from God?
- Do I ever struggle with the fear that my dreams may not be possible any longer?
- Am I actively looking for ways to honor God and give Him glory, even in the areas of my life that aren't going according to my plans?

ABRAHAM

And finally, from Abraham we learned how important it is to live every day of our lives in expectation of God's promises. Abraham's life was far from perfect. He made multiple mistakes while waiting for God to fulfill his dream.

At the beginning he made the same mistake as Hannah, asking for a single son, when God wanted him to become the father of multitudes. Then, after years of waiting he got frustrated and manufactured a carnal solution to his problem, just like Moses did. He also failed to maintain the same passion and zeal that Caleb had while waiting. When God told him that it was time for his dream to come true, he was so surprised he laughed in disbelief.

But Abraham did get one thing right. Once God convinced him that He was serious about giving him a son, Abraham put all of his doubting and second guessing behind him. From that moment forward, he lived his life in genuine anticipation of a move of God. He woke up every day fully expecting that his miracle was going to happen. As a result, the next time God came to visit Abraham, it didn't take him by surprise. In fact, he was already at the door of his tent, looking out as if he'd been expecting the Lord to arrive!

I pray that the expectation that Abraham demonstrated is stirring in your heart as well. Do not let the mistakes that you made in your past define your vision of your future. Do not look at your tomorrow with the assumption that it will be like your yesterday. Live every day in expectation that God is going to do great and wonderful things in your life. Wake up every morning and look for the hand of the Lord moving on your behalf. Choose today to live in expectation of a move of God. If it hasn't come yet, if you've been waiting a while, don't dismay! It only means that you are that-much-closer to realizing the dreams that He has placed in your heart.

Are you living your life in expectation of the fulfillment of your dreams? Here are a few questions that you can ask yourself to find out:

- Do I honestly believe that God is going to give me the dreams and desires in my heart?
- Do my everyday words and actions reflect that belief?
- Have I learned from and let go of the mistakes of my past? Or do I secretly believe that they may hold me back from achieving my dreams?
- Am I ready to move forward into my future?
- Am I actively looking for the opportunity to see my dream realized?
- What one word would I use to describe my perspective regarding my dream?

YOU

I would like to finish our discussion of dreams with this simple reminder: God has made you to be more than just a dreamer. You were made to be a dream chaser. He did not design you to be ordinary, commonplace, or average. He formed you on purpose, and then He gave you a destiny to fulfill. The dreams that God has placed in your heart are not an accident. They are intentional. They exist for a purpose. They are meant to push, provoke, and inspire you towards greatness.

However, like every blessing that comes from the Lord, our dreams bring with them a responsibility. We are responsible to actively pursue our dreams, to push towards them, to claim them, and to make them a reality.

Then Joshua said to the children of Israel: "How long will you neglect to go and possess the land which the Lord God of your fathers has given you?" (Joshua 18:3)

I think that sometimes as Christians we can get a little bit lazy when it comes to the things that God has promised us. We have developed a strange expectation: that if a dream or a promise comes from Him it should come to us easily, falling into our laps without any effort on our part. Of course we cannot earn or win our blessings from God by natural efforts. They are a free gift. But just because God has given you something does not negate your responsibility to get up and go get it! So what are you waiting for?

In the book of Joshua the Israelites were finally, after hundreds of years, released to go and claim the land that God had promised Abraham so many generations earlier. They had waited and suffered for their entire lives, believing that their dream would eventually become a reality. After forty years of wandering through the wilderness, God had finally commanded them to go and possess their promise. The Israelites heard His voice, and they obeyed , but only up to a point.

They had razed cities, conquered kings, slaughtered nations of people, and taken over huge territories. However, that was only the beginning of what God had in store for His people. He had promised them all of the land of Canaan, not just part of it. But somewhere along the way the people had lost their momentum. They'd lost their drive to complete the task that God had put before them. They settled for what they had already achieved. They neglected to possess the place that God had given them – content to leave it in the hands of the cursed people whom God had marked for destruction.

There are too many times in the lives of Christians when our God-given dreams stand in front of us, waiting to be claimed, only to be left there because we don't have the will or the character to do the work necessary to claim them. There are too many times when we have neglected the good and beautiful things that God has offered to us, simply because we don't feel prepared to exert the effort necessary to possess them.

So I would like to end this book by encouraging you not to be like the Israelites in this story. Don't allow your dreams to lie dormant. Don't let any excuse stop you from standing up and claiming the dream that God has given you.

If you are ready to chase you dream with all that is in you, start by challenging yourself with one last set of questions:

- What good and beautiful dream has God placed within your heart?
- What is it that you are supposed to be conquering in the name of the Lord?
- Have you lost sight of the purpose that had brought you to this point and place in your life?
- If so, how long will you neglect to possess the things that the Lord your God has given you?

Don't neglect your dreams any longer. Have the courage and the character to live every day in pursuit of what God is offering you. Allow your dreams to drive you to greatness. Dare to live your life as more than a dreamer. Arise and become the dream chaser that God has called you to be.

www.ingramcontent.com/pod-product-compliance
Lightning Source LLC
LaVergne TN
LVHW051408080426
835508LV00022B/2989

* 9 7 8 0 6 9 2 3 1 1 0 7 3 *